P

salad days

salad days

Boost Your Health and Happiness with 75 Simple,
Satisfying Recipes for Greens, Grains, Proteins, and More

—————————————

AMY PENNINGTON

SASQUATCH BOOKS

SEATTLE

EDITOR | Susan Roxborough

PRODUCTION EDITOR | Emma Reh

DESIGN | Anna Goldstein and Tony Ong

PHOTOGRAPHY | Charity Burggraaf

FOOD STYLING | Renee Beaudoin and
Charity Burggraaf

COPYEDITOR | Kristin Vorce Duran

Printed in China

Published by Sasquatch Books

21 20 19 18 17   9 8 7 6 5 4 3 2 1

Library of Congress Cataloging-in-Publication Data is available.

ISBN: 978-1-63217-085-9

Sasquatch Books
1904 Third Avenue, Suite 710
Seattle, WA 98101
(206) 467-4300
www.sasquatchbooks.com
custserv@sasquatchbooks.com

CONTENTS

INTRODUCTION

CAN A SALAD MAKE YOU HAPPY? I would like to think so. Salads, by nature, are healthy and clean, and there is a peaceful cadence and stillness to experience in preparing a meal. It's often one of the few times during the day I get to focus on a singular, intuitive task that results in nurturing my body and perhaps even those of my family and friends. What more can you ask for in the day? All the salads in this book will fuel you. With no heavy ingredients to weigh you down, the recipes in *Salad Days* supply you with delicious, pretty, and healthy salads to enrich your life. Slow down, take ten minutes, reflect on all the beautiful things in your life, and then sit and enjoy the process of self-nurturing by way of a well-prepared meal.

In recent years, salads have moved from side-dish afterthoughts to main meals. Parents are looking for healthy choices that are easy-to-whip-together crowd-pleasers, while single-person households are often reaching for healthy choices that don't require a lot of time in the kitchen. Here, I've channeled all of my salad prowess into one go-to cookbook for anyone wanting to add more veggies to their diet and for all home cooks in need of some fresh, seasonal salad ideas. Salads are one of those quintessential in-a-food-rut dishes. Bagged salad greens get tossed in a store-bought dressing with little thought to texture or flavor. Often, a salad is used solely as a way to add greens to a diet. *Salad Days* hopes to help break this pattern and offer readers a yearlong guide to healthy and seasonal salads that can be eaten as sides or treated as a complete meal.

Salad Days is approachable and applicable to life—no one needs another fancy cookbook with obscure ingredients. *Salad Days* uses typical pantry ingredients as well as trending favorites (miso, fish sauce, etc.) that can be found in For the Pantry (page 7), and it teaches people how to build on concepts to create their own salad.

On their own, vegetables are not really that captivating. Tasty? Yes. Those natural sugars and strong fibers are interesting, and their health benefits compelling, but seldom do you bite into a leaf of lettuce and roll your eyes in ecstasy.

To really dial up the flavor in a salad, we add herbs, spices, and toppings or make flavor-bomb vinaigrettes. Herein lies the magic of this book. Don't spend too much time fretting over whether you have a certain lettuce on hand—the best part is the additions. *Salad Days* is packed with tips. Any time you fire up the oven, throw a few cloves of garlic onto a roasting sheet for some future dressing, like the Garlic Oil Farro, Roasted Shiitake, and Pecorino (page 42). If the oven is on, you may as well multitask to build up your salad pantry and make good use of the energy you're consuming. If you're making candied pecans for one salad, make a double batch so there are extras to throw on a salad later that month. When you start working in this fashion, planning for meals no longer becomes a huge project.

There is one crucial and universal rule to keep in mind when making a salad. Acids and liquid break down greens quickly, so plan ahead. If you're prepping all the ingredients ahead of time, don't stir in the salad greens until immediately before serving. If you know you'll have leftovers (such as if you're a two-person household), split the recipes in half and add greens just before eating. Beans will hold in the refrigerator for days—dressed greens will not.

Homemade vinaigrettes and dressings are my favorite salad-making addition—changing up the oil or acid is a simple act that produces delightful results. I love them so much I included an entire chapter (see

page 180) with foundational ideas you can expand on, moving from simple vinaigrettes to creamy dressings. A bowl of greens can be boring, but dress it one day with lemon and oil and the next with a rich blend of avocado-miso, and you'll soon see just how captivating salads can be.

Typically I like a well-dressed salad, and the recipes here will reflect that. I don't like salad greens to wilt and turn slimy, nor do I like a thick coating of dressing on a tender green. However, I equally dislike when I eat a forkful of raw lettuce with nary the flavor of vinaigrette! I like to think all the recipes here strike a balance and everything is perfectly dressed. Additionally, extra vinaigrette in the bowl doesn't bother me, and I make a habit of saving any leftover dressing, adding it to a jar in the refrigerator for the next salad.

All vinaigrettes pretty much follow the same math—acid plus oil plus spices, and in this way, the flavors build on each other and morph as new ingredients are added. Think of this as a vinaigrette starter. This is especially true of fruit salads—berries, mangoes, and tomatoes all release their juices into the vinaigrette and leave behind a gentle acid and a fruity flavor that is a shame to wash away at the end of the meal. The only time I don't save leftovers is if I'm making a creamy dressing. Those have a different flavor profile and won't blend as seamlessly, so be sure to dress the salad and add more dressing only as needed. Any leftover dressing can often be held in the refrigerator, and notes on this are given through the chapters.

After you've nailed the dressing and have a pantry full of goodies to toss onto salads, you don't want to overlook the veg. The world of salad greens is plentiful—check out the note on overarching families of leafy options in Fast and Fresh Salads (page 116). Store-bought greens can be limiting, so keep your eyes open for any local farmers' markets and swing by a natural food store or co-op a few times a month for what is typically the freshest produce. Rotating where you shop will more easily offer a greater selection month over month.

I encourage anyone with space and sunlight to grow their own salad greens. Homegrown lettuce is an incomparable ingredient that cannot be replicated elsewhere. And for anyone without sun, try your hand at sprouting some greens on the countertop of your kitchen (see page 170). Sprouts are one of the most nutritious vegetables we can eat, and I highly recommend experimenting with them: adding them to green salads, grain bowls, or bean salads or using them as a pretty garnish on a salad you make for friends.

Truly, any vegetable can be used to compose a salad. Roasted, sautéed, mashed, or raw, vegetables add flavor, texture, and nutrients and can be added to bowls of grain or noodle or eaten on their own tossed with greens. *Salad Days* offers you several different ideas of what a salad can be, hoping to lend a hand in getting out of any habits and cooking ruts you've adopted.

And that's just what *Salad Days* aims to do—offer you a salad option for any occasion. Looking to add more fresh vegetables to your meals? Check! Want to start incorporating a meatless Monday? Check! Need some options for when there are slim pickings at the market? Check. Friends coming for dinner and you don't want to spend gobs of money? Check!

FOR THE PANTRY

THE FOLLOWING IS A LIST OF the pantry goods that I always keep handy for salad making. I vary my oils according to a desired flavor and consistency and sometimes at my whim. Same with the vinegars—sometimes I want a soft vinegar bite so I'll choose rice wine vinegar. Other days, for a zingier dressing, I'll grab my homemade apple cider vinegar. Other ingredients in the pantry add big flavor or texture to salads and will often act as inspiration from which to start off a recipe. In particular I love the emulsifiers which make for thick, rich dressings fit for noodle salads and grain bowls. A note about olive oil: when I find a splurge-worthy bottle of olive oil (they can easily run $30 a bottle), I buy that and use it only for simple green salads that are dressed solely with the oil and a splash of vinegar.

OILS

EXTRA-VIRGIN OLIVE OIL Hands down the oil I use the most for salads, dressing, finishing, roasting, cooking—you name it. Keep both a pricier, greener-tasting olive oil and a more affordable everyday olive oil in the cupboard. For simple salads and finishing oil, opt for the better-tasting olive oil, which should be peppery and fresh. Often, you will feel a little dryness in the back of your throat as you taste. Gourmet shops will offer tastings, which are a great way to select what you like. For flavorful salads, roasted veg, or large salads, use the everyday oil, which is cheaper. California oils are decent—if you have the chance, choose a smaller company, not the Goliaths whose oils tend to taste utterly neutral and disinteresting.

AVOCADO OIL My new favorite oil, avocado oil is heat tolerant and very light. A healthier option than other neutral vegetable oil, avocado oil is also very affordable.

PUMPKIN SEED OIL This oil tastes exactly like a toasted pumpkin seed. Its nutty and mild flavor is very compelling and adds some weight to salads. Choose pumpkin seed oil for seasoning and dressing your winter greens and roasted vegetable salads, but don't cook with it— it's not known to be a heat-tolerant oil.

SESAME SEED OIL A must-have for Asian-inspired dressings, this oil lends a nutty, toasty quality that is otherwise hard to replicate.

VINEGARS

APPLE CIDER VINEGAR This vinegar is pungent yet sweet—it's my go-to vinegar for pretty much everything I make. It's made from fermented apple cider, and you can make homemade apple cider vinegar (see page 10) through home fermentation, making a live product that is wonderful for colon health.

RED WINE VINEGAR A go-to for vinaigrettes, red wine vinegar has a sharp bite that wakes up not-very-flavorful ingredients like grains or bean salads.

RICE WINE VINEGAR This gentle vinegar packs an acidic bite while also having a soft sweetness. I use rice wine vinegar in quick pickles, Asian dressings, and even in vinaigrettes for simple green salads.

SHERRY VINEGAR Produced in the same area of Spain where sherry is made, sherry vinegar is aged vinegar made in casks. It is sweet and slightly woody in flavor—a very nice vinegar paired with strong leafy greens and any salad with cooked proteins or grains. Sherry vinegar is also a lovely vinegar for pickling fruit, both fresh and dried.

EMULSIFIERS

AVOCADO Purchase hard avocados that are firm if you'd like to use them in three days. For immediate use, choose avocados that give slightly when lightly pressed. At the grocery store I opt for one of each so when one avocado is finished, I have another just coming in to ripeness. Pureed with a bit of liquid, avocados make a smooth and velvety dressing that thickly coats greens and adds creaminess to grain bowls.

CHIA GEL Chia seeds are high in omega-3 fats and fiber. The flavor of chia seeds is not strong—it's more about the texture. Through absorption of an added liquid, chia seeds create a gelatinous exterior, similar to that of tapioca in pudding or bubble tea. If you like this toothsome, custard-like quality, chia is a win. To make gel, add a spoonful of chia to three parts water and store it in the refrigerator, adding spoonfuls to vinaigrettes or blended dressings for thickness and texture.

MISO Miso is a thick paste made from fermented soybean. It can be quite sweet, salty, and pungent and varies in flavor and texture across brands. White or light-colored miso is mild in flavor, and it's the type used most often in this book. The darker the miso, the stronger the flavor, which can be a blessing to some and off-putting to others. As a fermented product, miso is live and contains beneficial probiotics, so in addition to being a flavorful element to salad dressings, miso adds a healthy pop of immunity-boosting properties to recipes.

NUT BUTTERS Creamy nut butters can be used for both their texture and nutritional value in salads. Their thick, rich quality lends itself well to dressings that coat greens, grains, and noodles alike. Choose a nut butter based on your preferences—all will work well. Often, I opt for cashew butter, due to its mild flavor and smooth texture, while peanut butter is my first choice for Asian-inspired sauces and meals.

TAHINI A thick paste made from ground sesame seed, tahini adds a toasty, nutty flavor to dressings that is similar to nut butters. Tahini tends to be slightly thinner than nut butters and is, therefore, a lighter option when you want to thickly coat greens.

YOGURT Plain yogurt can take the place of mayonnaise, sour cream, or crème fraîche in dressings, replacing the fat calories with a leaner option. A live-culture yogurt will also contribute probiotics to your diet, which are wonderful for gut health. Opt for plain nonfat yogurt when you want a low-calorie dressing that is creamy.

HOMEMADE APPLE CIDER VINEGAR

APPLE CIDER VINEGAR IS A SOFT, round vinegar that is slightly sweet. It is fairly easy to make your own apple cider vinegar at home. You can use scraps from apples—the cores and skins make great starters. Of course, you can use whole apples as well; just be sure to choose ripe ones, as they have a higher sugar content than unripe apples, allowing for a slightly sweeter product in the end. Choosing bruised apples, called seconds, at the farmers' market is an affordable option.

This recipe forgoes any formal procuring of brewer's yeast, casks, and equipment, and sticks to using materials found in most homes. Use a large nonreactive pot for this project—a large stainless-steel pot or a deep earthenware pot work well.

With vinegar-making, oxygen needs to be present—in order for alcohol to turn to vinegar, it needs air. Oxygen on a liquid's surface will help bacteria in the process of converting alcohol to acetic acid, (the vinegar). You must watch for mold forming on the surface of your solution. Mold is an indication that the balance of acid to sugar is off; it generally will not form if the balance is right. In the event that mold presents itself on the apples' surface, skim it off and keep an eye on the apples. Your nose, too, will be a good indicator if something goes awry. Home fermentation should smell boozy and pungent, not off-putting. If mold develops a second time, toss the batch and start over—something may be off. This recipe makes about 1 quart of vinegar.

TO MAKE THE VINEGAR:

▸ In the large pot or earthenware container, put the cores and peels from ten apples (or five whole apples, finely chopped). In a 5-quart bowl, dissolve ¼ cup of sugar in the water and pour it over the apple scraps; they should be covered completely. If they are not, make another mixture of 4 cups water and ¼ cup sugar and add to the pot, but only enough to cover apples. Discard any leftover sweetened water.

▸ Cover the top of the pot with four layers of thick cheesecloth secured with kitchen twine, and set it in a warm spot in the kitchen. The interior of a cupboard works well, as does a countertop. (If you're making vinegar in summer, secure the cheesecloth tightly to prevent fruit flies from getting into the pot and laying eggs, which will spoil the batch.)

▸ Leave the mixture for 1 week to macerate and ferment. The liquid may darken slightly and the apple mash will bubble—all signs of a good fermentation. After a week, strain out the apple mash from the liquid by setting it in a mesh strainer over a deep pot and allowing the mash to sit for 24 hours. Do not press on the solids to extract more liquid.

▸ Return the apple liquid to the container and cover it again with a thick layer of cheesecloth. Put the container in a warm spot and let it sit for 2 to 3 weeks, allowing the sugars to convert to vinegar. Stir or swirl the liquid every few days, to allow for air circulation and oxygen.

▸ After 2 weeks, taste a spoonful of your vinegar for doneness. If the vinegar still tastes fruity and not acidic enough, let it sit for another week and taste again. After 3 weeks total, the liquid should be completely converted to apple cider vinegar.

▸ To store apple cider vinegar, strain the liquid with a fine mesh sieve and pour it into clean, sterilized glass bottles. Store vinegar in a cool, dark place. Do not use homemade vinegar in canned goods, as acidity levels vary with each batch. Apple cider vinegar keeps indefinitely.

ADD-ONS

DRIED FRUITS Dried figs, dates, apricots, and raisins are excellent pantry staples. In combination, dried fruits work together in baked goods or as sides to main courses. On their own, they are sweet additions to savory salads.

FISH SAUCE Made from salted, fermented fish, this condiment brings a welcome punch to vinaigrettes and dressings. Because fish sauce falls outside the flavor categories typically recognized by the American palate, the savory-salty taste is hard to define. The Japanese describe it as *umami*—roughly translated as *deliciousness*. A versatile pantry staple, fish sauce imparts a noticeable difference in recipes.

FLAVORED NUTS Toasted in oil and tossed in sugar, candied nuts add crispness and sweetness to salads and in particular work well with bitter greens. Throw in a spoonful of soy sauce, and you have sweet-salty. Add a small pinch of cayenne, and you have some spice. Try the recipe for Candied Pecans (page 129) for any nut, and vary the spices as you see fit.

KIMCHI A fermented cabbage, kimchi is good and good for you. Often tasting strongly of chili and garlic, kimchi adds flavor and healthy probiotics to meals. As kimchi is already fermented, it keeps for a long while, so even if you're not going to eat it every day, it's smart to keep a jar handy for occasional use.

NORI These dark sheets of pressed seaweed can be torn, chopped, and flaked and used as garnish for salads. Nori has an earthy, sweet taste and thick, papery texture that melts in your mouth. Very high in protein, vitamins, and iodine, nori is a wonderful addition to grain bowls and salads, particularly for vegetarians looking to up their daily protein intake.

NUTS Keep a selection of dried nuts in the pantry in small quantities, which helps ensure they will not go rancid with age. For any large quantity of nuts, store them tightly wrapped in plastic in the freezer. I prefer raw nuts so I can either soak them for dressings (which keeps the flavor neutral, not toasted) or toast them as I like, for salad toppings, pestos, or toasted dressings. My standards are pistachio, almond, pine nut, and hazelnut for salads, though I try to keep one cup of all nuts in my pantry at all times.

QUICK PICKLES There are two techniques to make a quick pickle: In the first, you heat pickling liquid (along with aromatics and sugar) and pour it over the prepared vegetable or fruit; in the second, you simply throw everything into a bowl and let it cure in vinegar by giving it a stir once in a while. Quick pickles are vegetables or fruits that pickle in about twenty minutes or less. This short brine time leaves the pickles crispy and vibrantly colored, adding texture, color, and flavor to a dish. Anything can be pickled—thin slices of shallot or ginger, dried raisins, or slices of jalapeño or apples are delicious additions to salads.

SEED MIX I keep a small jar of blended seeds in the pantry for a salad topper—a collection of seeds adds flavor and crunch. Whole spice seeds (anise, fennel) add loads of flavor. My favorite combination is toasted sesame seeds, aniseeds, and black poppy seeds, blended with a generous heap of coarse salt. Use this to sprinkle on salads or over grain bowls.

SMOKED FISH Whether fleshy slices of smoked salmon, thin flakes of smoked trout, or big hunks of dry mackerel, smoked fish is an easy choice for adding flavor and protein to a salad. Smoked fish keeps for quite some time, so I always have some on hand for quick and healthy meals when I don't have time to think about or plan what I'm eating.

breakfast salads

IF YOU'RE EATING LEAN AND CLEAN, salad is a great way to start the day. My daily goal is to eat as many vegetables as possible. Veggies fill you up, add mega nutrients to your diet, and are healthy carbohydrates needed for fuel all day long. Making a big salad at every meal is a no-brainer, even for breakfast.

A bowl of kimchi and a soft-boiled egg is one of my standards, as is a fried egg over simply dressed greens. I'll eat whatever I have on hand—every green I can think of goes well with oozy egg yolk, acid, and oil. And while those simple salads are excellent options, there are ways to fancy it up a bit for days when you have extra time or will linger over a brunch.

Breakfast salads need not be all greens. Roasted tomatoes spill from a piece of thickly sliced rustic bread on the Tomato Chip and Mozzarella Toast (page 21). Sure, you can add a handful of arugula, but on its own it is just as delicious. Equally satisfying is a bowl of roasted beets and soft-boiled egg. Beets are naturally sweet, and there is something about the earthy sugar that appeals first thing in the morning.

And don't forget the power of leftovers to inform your morning meal—they can be turned into a breakfast salad plate. Think roasted sweet potatoes, salad greens lightly dressed, and a fried egg for protein, and you've got a balanced, nutritional meal in minutes.

MAPLE BACON
with Frilly Greens and Fried Egg

This simple breakfast pairs sweet syrup-encrusted bacon with a skillet-fried egg and salad greens. It is the lazy person's *frisée aux lardon*! So the sugars in the syrup don't burn, this bacon is cooked in the oven to a chewy consistency. If you're a crispy bacon lover, increase your oven temperature slightly and monitor for doneness. Whichever your preference, line your pan with aluminum foil to spare a messy clean up. Here, I prefer a fried egg, as I cook it until the edges are lacy and crisp, but you can easily substitute a poached egg, soft-boiled egg, etc. Work quickly so the greens don't break down too much and the bacon is still warm as you serve it.

MAKES 4 SERVINGS

4 slices thick-cut bacon
1 tablespoon maple syrup
6 cups lettuce greens
   (frisée, escarole, oakleaf)
2 tablespoons extra-virgin
   olive oil, plus more
   for frying
1 tablespoon apple
   cider vinegar
Kosher salt and freshly
   ground black pepper
4 large eggs

▶ Preheat the oven to 350 degrees F.
▶ On a large baking sheet, place the bacon slices in a single layer making sure they do not touch. Drizzle the maple syrup evenly over them and bake until the bacon is cooked to your liking, 20 to 25 minutes. Set aside until ready to use.
▶ In a large bowl, toss the lettuce greens, oil, and vinegar until well combined. Season to taste with salt and pepper and portion evenly into four shallow bowls. Set aside.
▶ Meanwhile, cover the bottom of a large sauté pan with oil and heat over medium high. When the oil begins to ripple slightly, crack in the eggs. Cook for 3 to 4 minutes, until the outer edges of the whites are crispy and brown. Use a spatula to flip the eggs yolk-side down and cook for 2 minutes more, making sure to leave the yolks runny.
▶ To serve, place the egg directly over the salad greens, and place one piece of bacon in each of the four bowls. Serve immediately.

CHEESY POLENTA AND CHARRED GREENS
with Crispy Prosciutto

Cornmeal (a.k.a. grits or polenta) cooks up very quickly and has a creamy texture and corn-like flavor—it's an ideal grain for a savory morning porridge. Here, polenta is cooked and then tossed with cheese, while bitter greens are charred under the broiler. Topped with crisp prosciutto, this is a super hearty and healthy breakfast that is easy enough for the workweek but a fabulous dish for a lazy weekend brunch no matter how many people you are trying to serve at once.

MAKES 4 SERVINGS

3 cups water, chicken or vegetable broth, or milk (or a combination of the three)
1 cup coarse cornmeal
¼ cup freshly grated Parmesan
2 tablespoons unsalted butter
½ teaspoon kosher salt
¼ teaspoon freshly ground black pepper
4 cups bitter greens, escarole, or radicchio, cut into ½-inch ribbons
3 tablespoons extra-virgin olive oil
4 slices prosciutto
Maple syrup, for garnish (optional)

▶ In a medium saucepan over medium-high heat, bring the water to a boil. Add the cornmeal, a little bit at a time, whisking to incorporate. Lower the heat to medium low and stir frequently and rigorously, cooking for about 15 minutes, or until the polenta is softened and thick. Remove from the heat and add the Parmesan, butter, salt, and pepper. Cover and set aside for 5 to 10 minutes to rest.

▶ Preheat the broiler.

▶ On a large baking sheet, spread out the ribbons of greens and drizzle with the oil. Toss to coat the greens and set the pan under the broiler to char the greens, 3 to 4 minutes. Some edges should be very dark and crispy, while others will be soft. Remove from the oven and set aside.

▶ In a medium sauté pan, lay the prosciutto, taking care not to overlap the slices. Cook until brown and crispy on one side, 1 to 2 minutes, then flip. Brown the other side, a minute or so more, and remove from the heat. Let the prosciutto cool slightly and break into large pieces.

▶ To assemble individual servings, in a shallow bowl, put the polenta and cover with a heap of greens. Add a few crumbles of prosciutto. Drizzle with maple syrup and serve immediately.

TOMATO CHIP AND MOZZARELLA TOAST

This was one of my favorite breakfasts as a kid, although I've updated it here with roasted tomatoes instead of fresh. Melted mozzarella on a thick hunk of bread is comfort food made for a morning meal, and super-dehydrated tomatoes are a thing of beauty. Their flavor is deeply pronounced and, if you time it right, the edges offer a charred taste with a chewy texture that feels like taffy on your teeth, but it's savory. Layer them all together, and this breakfast is addictive. Make the tomatoes overnight or the evening before so they are ready to go in the morning.

MAKES 4 SERVINGS

12 roma tomatoes or other paste tomatoes
¼ cup extra-virgin olive oil
3 tablespoons chopped fresh thyme
Kosher salt
4 thick slices of rustic bread
4 ounces fresh mozzarella, thinly sliced

▶ Preheat the oven to 175 degrees F.
▶ Cut the tomatoes into even slices—no fatter than ½ inch thick. Place the tomato slices in a single layer on a baking sheet, leaving a bit of space between the edges, and drizzle them evenly with oil. Sprinkle with the thyme and salt very lightly. Roast in the oven until the tomatoes are crispy and completely dry, 3 to 6 hours. Remove from the oven.
▶ To compose the toast, preheat the broiler. On a baking sheet, lightly toast the first side, 3 to 4 minutes. Turn the bread over, and lay the mozzarella slices over the top evenly across all four pieces. Return to the oven and broil until the mozzarella is melted and begins to bubble and darken slightly, about 3 minutes more. Remove from the oven and layer a generous amount of tomato chips across all four toasts. Drizzle with any residual oil from the baking sheet and serve.

PROBIOTIC SALAD—KIMCHI DRESSING AND GREENS
with Avocado and Sweet Potato Fries

Fermented foods offer us live cultures that are great for the gut—natural probiotics we can have as our meals. I make a habit of starting my day with them. Here, kimchi—a Korean fermented cabbage with chili—is pureed with miso (another cultured product), yogurt (more live cultures!), and oil to make a smooth and creamy vinaigrette. Paired with fatty avocado and crispy sweet potato fries, this breakfast takes a little bit of time, but everything can be made in advance and tossed together in the morning. Vegans can sub out the yogurt for silken tofu with good results.

MAKES 4 SERVINGS

½ cup plain yogurt
¼ cup kimchi
¼ cup white miso
1 tablespoon rice wine vinegar
1 tablespoon fish sauce
½ cup avocado oil
¼ cup coconut oil
2 medium sweet potatoes, peeled and diced
Kosher salt
6 cups mixed lettuce greens
1 large avocado, sliced
Freshly ground black pepper

▶ In the bowl of a food processor or strong blender, put the yogurt, kimchi, miso, vinegar, and fish sauce. With the machine running on high, slowly drizzle in the avocado oil until the vinaigrette is emulsified, about 30 seconds. Set aside until ready to use.

▶ In a large sauté pan over medium-high heat, melt the coconut oil. When the oil is hot and showing ripples, place a single layer of the sweet potato cubes in the pan and sprinkle with salt. Cook, stirring only occasionally, until all sides are golden brown, 7 to 10 minutes. Remove from the heat and set aside to cool.

▶ To compose the salad, in a large bowl, put the greens. Add a few spoonfuls of dressing, the avocado, and the sweet potato fries. Stir until all are well coated and combined, adding more dressing as you like. Season to taste with salt and pepper and serve.

ROASTED BEETS AND BEET GREEN SALSA VERDE
with Egg

Roasted beets and their green tops are loaded with vitamin A and carotenoids—anti-infection vitamins that support healthy immune systems. Here, the beet root is roasted and the greens are used in a spicy green salsa, similar to pesto but with way more heat. An egg on top provides needed protein to start your day. To measure the cilantro, simply fold up the whole stem and twirl it into a measuring cup. Or simply grab a handful and add it in—you can adjust the proportion up or down easily by adding more ingredients.

▶ Preheat the oven to 425 degrees F.
▶ Scrub the beets free of all dirt, peel the roots, remove the beet greens, and reserve five leaves. In a shallow baking dish, put the beets, toss them with 2 tablespoons of the oil, and season to taste with salt and pepper. Cover the baking dish with aluminum foil and roast until the beets can be pierced through the center with a knife but are still firm, 50 to 60 minutes. Set aside, and when they are cool enough to handle, cut the beet root into wedges. Place equal amounts across four small bowls.
▶ Trim the stems from the reserved beet greens. In a blender on medium speed, blend the greens, jalapeño, onions, cilantro, water, and the remaining 4 tablespoons oil until the consistency is paste-like and loose enough to pour. If it is too thick, add a few more spoonfuls of oil and stir. Set aside.
▶ To make the soft-boiled eggs, bring a medium saucepan of water to a boil over high heat. Using a spoon, gently drop the eggs into the water and reduce the heat to a low simmer. Cook for exactly 6 minutes, resulting in a medium-set egg wherein the yolk will be set, but oozy, and the whites will be firm, but not rubbery. Strain the eggs from the saucepan and run under cool water until cool enough to handle and peel. Add one egg to each bowl, and slice in half, drizzling a generous amount of salsa verde over each.

MAKES 4 SERVINGS

4 to 6 medium red beets, greens attached
6 tablespoons extra-virgin olive oil, divided, plus more as needed
Kosher salt and freshly ground black pepper
½ medium jalapeño
2 green onions, roots trimmed
1 cup fresh cilantro leaves and stems
1 tablespoon water
4 large eggs

WARM KALE AND BACON
with Sweet Corn

Warmed vinaigrette partially cooks the kale in this salad, softening the leaves. Corn kernels add a sweet, crisp bite, and bacon gives it a pleasant, smoky flavor. A good salad in summer when corn is fresh or winter when kale is one of the few green options, this salad is a yearlong winner. The sherry vinegar delivers a punch that is well needed in this fatty, rich salad. If you don't have sherry vinegar, opt for red wine vinegar instead.

MAKES 4 SERVINGS

1 bunch kale, stemmed and cut into 1-inch ribbons
½ pound thick bacon, cut into 1-inch pieces
¼ cup finely chopped shallot
Kosher salt and freshly ground black pepper
1 cup fresh or frozen and thawed corn kernels
2 tablespoons sherry vinegar
1 tablespoon extra-virgin olive oil
4 ounces shaved Parmesan

▶ In a large bowl, put the kale and set aside.

▶ In a large skillet over medium-high heat, cook the bacon until brown and crisp, stirring occasionally, 6 to 8 minutes. Remove the pan from the heat, pour off and reserve the bacon fat, and transfer the bacon to paper towels to cool slightly.

▶ Return the skillet to medium-high heat and add 2 tablespoons of the reserved bacon fat and the shallots. Season to taste with salt and pepper and cook, stirring often, until the shallots have softened and turned translucent, about 2 minutes. Add the corn to pan and cook, undisturbed, until the corn starts to brown, about 2 minutes. Stir once and let it sit, putting half the kale over the corn while the other side browns, for about 2 minutes more.

▶ Remove the skillet from the heat and add the vinegar and oil, scraping up any brown bits from the skillet. Stir continuously until the kale is wilted. Pour the warm kale and vinaigrette into the bowl with the rest of the kale and toss to combine well. Add the bacon and Parmesan, season to taste with salt and pepper, and serve.

ASPARAGUS AND EGG SAUCE

Eggs and asparagus are a natural pairing that turns up on breakfast and dinner menus alike. This recipe skips an omelette and fried eggs for *gribiche*, a cold mayo-like sauce that uses hard-boiled eggs as the emulsifier. It's thick, oily, herby, and delicious. While seemingly complicated, the sauce comes together in minutes and asparagus steams equally quick, so this is an easy meal for a crowd and provides some wow factor. The sauce can be made to your own tastes as well—maybe add more chopped pickle or mix up the herbs. For an extra hearty breakfast, serve alongside a hunk of smoked fish—I'd go with smoked and flaked herring.

MAKES 4 SERVINGS

1 hard-boiled egg, yolk separated and whites diced
1 teaspoon Dijon mustard
¼ cup extra-virgin olive oil
1 teaspoon red wine vinegar
1 tablespoon diced cucumber pickle or cornichon
1 tablespoon capers
¼ cup chopped fresh parsley or dill (or a combination of the two)
Kosher salt and freshly ground black pepper
1 pound asparagus, woody ends removed

▶ In a blender, put the egg yolk and mustard. With the blender running on high speed, drizzle in the oil to make a thick emulsion, 30 seconds to 1 minute. Scrape the mixture into a medium bowl.

▶ Fold in the vinegar, egg whites, pickles, capers, and herbs until well combined. Don't worry if the sauce breaks a little—it will be delicious. Season to taste with salt and pepper. Thin the sauce out with a few more drops of oil, if desired, and set aside.

▶ To steam the asparagus, bring a large pot of water to a boil over high heat and salt lightly. Once boiling, drop in the asparagus spears and cover, cooking until the asparagus is just tender and still bright green, 3 to 4 minutes. Remove the pot from the heat, strain the asparagus, and plate immediately, topping with a dollop of egg sauce to serve.

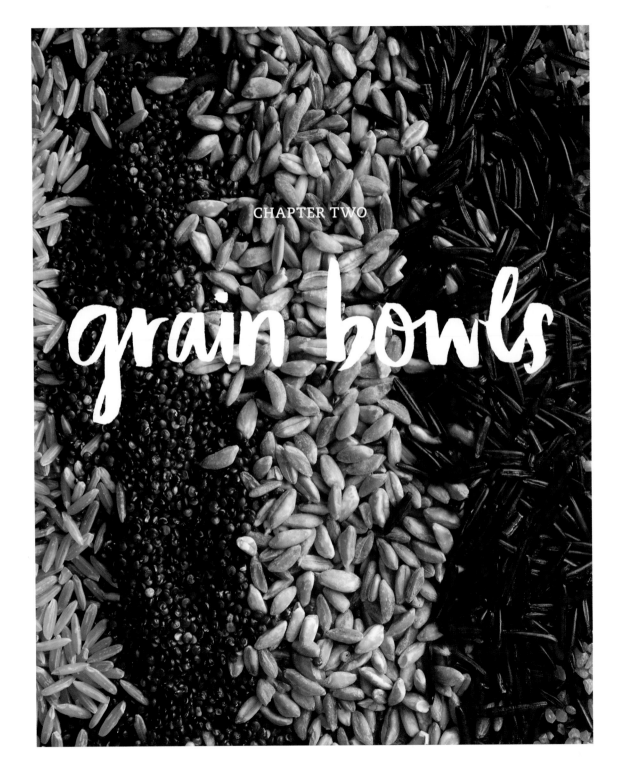

CHAPTER TWO

grain bowls

A HEARTY LUNCH OPTION, grain bowls take the satiating quality of whole grains and pair it with the freshness of a salad. Grain bowls are layered affairs—something steamed, something roasted, something fresh—that are married together with vinaigrette. They are perfect for packed lunches and midday fuel.

Whole grains are actual plant seeds. They are an excellent source of fiber and often protein, and are slowly metabolized by the body, leaving us feeling satisfied longer and contributing to stabilized blood sugar levels. It is widely accepted that whole grains, including those that are gluten-free, are paramount to a healthy diet and aid in the prevention of cancer, heart disease, and diabetes. Grain bowls can be absolute flavor bombs, packing in a new seasoning or spice with every component. Grains can be left plain or tossed in simple vinaigrettes—even tossing cooked grains in a good, peppery olive oil will alter the flavor profile subtly. Flavor accumulates as ingredients are added—whole or toasted spices, fried nuts, toothsome seeds, and more can be layered on for zing and intrigue.

TOASTED BULGUR
with Spicy Broccoli Rabe and Garlic Chips

Toasting grains before you steam them is a subtle way to introduce flavor into an otherwise unexciting grain—a bit of doctoring up really amplifies the flavor. Broccoli rabe (a.k.a. rapini) is similar to broccoli but has broad leaves and an appealing bitter flavor. Be sure to source these and not broccolini, which look similar but taste like broccoli and won't add much to the bowl. Adding a soft-boiled egg turns this into a more substantial meal.

MAKES 4 SERVINGS

2 cups uncooked bulgur wheat
3 cups boiling water
1 bunch broccoli rabe
10 cloves garlic, peeled and smashed
6 tablespoons extra-virgin olive oil, divided
Kosher salt and freshly ground black pepper
2 teaspoons red chili flakes
1 teaspoon lemon zest
½ cup golden raisins
3 tablespoons champagne vinegar
2 tablespoons honey
¼ cup roasted almonds, chopped

▶ Preheat the oven to 450 degrees F.
▶ Heat a large skillet over high heat. When the skillet is hot, toast the bulgur grains, stirring constantly, until lightly browned and fragrant, about 4 minutes. In a medium glass bowl, put the toasted bulgur and pour in the boiling water. Cover the bowl with plastic wrap or a plate and set aside to steam until all the water is absorbed and the grains are al dente, 20 to 25 minutes.
▶ While the bulgur is steaming, on a large baking sheet, put the broccoli rabe and garlic. Cover with 3 tablespoons of the oil, turning with your hands to coat thoroughly and evenly. Season liberally with salt and pepper and spread in a single layer on the baking sheet. Bake the broccoli rabe until charred and tender, about 20 minutes, turning once halfway through. Remove it from the oven and set aside to cool slightly. While the broccoli rabe is still warm, add the chili flakes and zest, tossing until well combined.
▶ Drain any additional water from the grains. Add the raisins, vinegar, honey, and the remaining 3 tablespoons oil to the bulgur and set aside until ready to use.
▶ To compose the bowls, put equal parts bulgur in each bowl and top with equal parts of broccoli rabe and garlic cloves. Scrape any residual oil from the baking sheet over the bowls. Sprinkle with almonds and serve.

RED QUINOA
with Crispy Kale, Charred Butternut Squash, and Cashew-Honey Dressing

Quinoa, when cooked, has an outer germ that breaks from the internal seed and provides firm, crispy texture. If left uncooked, quinoa can be eaten after soaking in liquid for a short period—doing this adds even more texture to the bowl and qualifies as a raw food. Here, squash is roasted until burned around the edges in a fiery chili sauce, while kale is roasted and crumbled into the salad as a flaky "chip." For a pop of protein, a thick cashew-based dressing is made slightly sweet with honey.

▸ Preheat the oven to 350 degrees F.

▸ To make the dressing, in a small bowl, put the cashews, water, honey, and cumin and let sit for 20 to 30 minutes. In a blender, puree the mixture until smooth and creamy. Season to taste with salt and pepper and set aside until ready to use.

▸ In a large bowl, put the squash pieces. Add the harissa, 2 tablespoons of the oil, and ½ teaspoon of the salt and toss to evenly coat. In a shallow roasting pan, place the squash, making sure the slices do not overlap. Scrape up any remaining harissa from the bowl and drizzle it over the squash pieces, then bake for 20 minutes. Remove the pan from the oven, toss the squash lightly to recoat with the harissa, and return the pan to the oven. Bake for 10 to 25 minutes more, until the squash is tender and the harissa starts to get crispy and thick.

▸ While the squash is roasting, steam the quinoa. In a medium pot with a lid over high heat, put the water and quinoa, cover, and bring to a boil. Reduce the heat to a simmer and cook for 12 to 15 minutes, or until all the liquid is absorbed. Remove the pot from heat, and allow the quinoa to continue steaming, covered, for about 10 minutes more.

MAKES 4 SERVINGS

FOR THE CASHEW-HONEY DRESSING:
½ cup raw cashews
¼ cup boiling water
1 teaspoon honey
¼ teaspoon ground cumin
Kosher salt and freshly ground black pepper

1 butternut squash, halved, seeded, cut into 2-inch-thick slices
3 tablespoons harissa
3 tablespoons extra-virgin olive oil, divided
1 teaspoon kosher salt, divided, plus more for seasoning
2 cups water
1½ cups red quinoa, rinsed until water runs clear
1 bunch kale, stemmed and torn into pieces
Freshly ground black pepper

▶ Meanwhile, in a large bowl, put the kale, the remaining 1 tablespoon oil, and remaining ½ teaspoon salt. Using your hands, toss to combine well so that all the pieces of kale are coated in oil. Massage the oil into the folds and crinkles of the kale and place it on two baking sheets in a single layer. (Make sure the edges of the kale do not overlap. You may need to bake in batches.) Put the baking sheets in the oven and roast until the kale is crispy but not charred, 15 to 20 minutes. Turn the kale chips over halfway through baking to help dry them out. Small pieces will cook faster, so remove any pieces that crisp up early. Remove the baking sheets from the oven and set the kale chips aside to cool for 1 or 2 minutes before serving.

▶ To make the individual servings, in a shallow bowl, put 1 cup of the quinoa. Place several slices of the squash on top, crumble several kale chips over them, drizzle with a quarter of the dressing, and serve. Season to taste with salt and pepper.

GRAIN BOWLS

SEED BOWL
with Wild Rice and Ginger Kale

My friend, the late Christina Choi, used to own a little café called Nettletown in Seattle where she turned out fusion food that was thoughtful, delicious, and healthy. In a world full of sandwiches for lunch, her café was a reprieve where I often had a quick meal between my garden work. One of my favorites was her Bhutan rice bowl—a simply steamed bowl of rice, seeds, dried seaweed, and sesame oil. Here is my homage to this dish, which I make when I want a simple, small, and satisfying vegetarian meal.

▶ Preheat the oven to 350 degrees F.
▶ In a medium pot over high heat, bring the water to a boil. Add the rice and bring back up to a boil. Cover, reduce the heat, and simmer until the rice is cooked through and splits, 45 to 60 minutes. Drain off any remaining water and set aside, keeping the cover on to continue steaming.
▶ In a large bowl, put the kale, olive oil, and ginger. Using your hands, toss to combine well so that all the pieces of kale are coated in oil. Massage the oil into the folds and crinkles of the kale. Add a few more drops of olive oil, if needed. Place the kale on two baking sheets in a single layer. (Make sure the edges of the kale do not overlap. You may need to bake in batches.) Season to taste with salt and pepper and put the baking sheets in the oven. Roast until the kale is crispy but not charred, 15 to 20 minutes. Turn the kale chips over halfway through baking to help dry them out. Small pieces will bake faster, so remove any pieces that crisp up early. Remove the baking sheets from the oven and set the kale chips aside to cool.
▶ In a small bowl, combine the sesame, poppy, anise, and fennel seeds with the chili flakes and salt.
▶ To compose the bowls, in a large bowl, put the sesame oil and the rice and stir well to coat. Put equal portions of the cooked rice in each bowl and top with equal portions of kale. Sprinkle with equal portions of the seed mix and serve.

MAKES 4 SERVINGS

2 cups water
1 cup wild rice
1 bunch kale, stemmed and torn into pieces
3 tablespoons extra-virgin olive oil
2 tablespoons grated fresh ginger
1 teaspoon kosher salt, plus more for seasoning
Freshly ground black pepper
1 tablespoon toasted sesame seeds
1 tablespoon poppy seed
1 tablespoon aniseed
1 tablespoon fennel seed
1 teaspoon red chili flakes
2 teaspoons sesame oil

ANATOMY OF THE GRAIN BOWL

IN THE ANATOMY OF A GRAIN BOWL, the grains provide the base layer and can be simply steamed or manipulated to offer flavor or texture. Add crispness to steamed grains by sautéing them with garlic and oil over high heat. Baking, too, lends a chewy mouthfeel to steamed grains—check out Herby Peas and Crispy Green Rice (page 45). For variety combine different grains. Try both quinoa and wild rice as a grain bowl base. Pulses, too, can be added to bulk up the meal—think millet with a spoonful of black beans or brown rice tossed with chickpeas.

You can add flavor by steaming grains with broth instead of water. Try adding a cupful of leftover wine to the broth, which furthers the savory flavor. Cooking water may also be infused with aromatics. Add citrus peels, dried spices, or fresh herbs to the pot.

From there, build. Greens come next and range from raw salad greens to crispy roasted kale leaves. Take advantage of cooking techniques to add texture. Roasting greens adds a crisp, burned flavor to the bowl, while steaming vegetables contributes pure flavor and creaminess. In summer add a handful of chopped fresh lettuce leaves and plenty of herbs. In winter rely on thinly sliced ribbons of cabbage or kale. Toss tough greens with vinaigrette first to help them soften, or leave them raw for a toothsome bite (like we do in Winter Salads with Lemongrass-Pistachio Brussels Sprouts and Lime-Soaked Leaves, page 54).

After the veg, add-ins and dressings can really make the bowl! Sliced chilies, crispy pieces of dried seaweed, flavorful puffed rice (like in Broccoli "Steaks" with Zucchini Hummus and Curried Puffed Rice, page 58), and pickled fruit and vegetables work beautifully. Add crunch to the bowl by way of seeds, sprouts (see Homegrown Sprouts, page 170), and nuts. Raw, toasted, or fried, these contribute both flavor and protein to grain bowls. Dried fruits add sweetness and texture—soak them in liquid first (sherry-infused raisins!) and you double up on flavor.

Options for grain bowls are seemingly endless, making them an excellent addition to the salad lineup.

QUINOA BOWL
with Curried Cauliflower, Pickled Raisins, and Beet-Tahini Dressing

This bowl packs big flavor and gets extra points for color—the beet-tahini dressing is bright fuchsia and will turn everything pink once stirred in. Like most bowls this one is composed of various layers, yet it is easy to make and comes together quickly. Use any leftover roasted vegetables from last night's dinner in place of the cauliflower, and you can have a meal on the table (or packed for an at-desk lunch) in minutes. If you have time and want to get fancy, use a pickling brine for the raisins—A+ for flavor.

▶ Preheat the oven to 350 degrees F.
▶ Peel the outer leaves from the cauliflower, setting them aside. Break off the cauliflower florets and cut the core into small chunks. On a large baking sheet, put the florets, core, and full leaves, leaving space between them so they're not overlapping much. Drizzle with the oil and season to taste with salt and pepper. Toss well so all the pieces are coated and roast for 30 minutes, until the cauliflower is crispy and brown. Check after 10 minutes and remove any leaves that are charred and burning. Remove from the oven and sprinkle the curry powder over the cauliflower, tossing to coat all the pieces evenly. Set aside.
▶ To steam the quinoa, in a medium pot with a lid over high heat, put the water and grains, cover, and bring to a boil. Reduce the heat to a simmer and cook for 12 to 15 minutes more, or until all the liquid is absorbed. Remove the pot from heat, and allow the quinoa to continue steaming, covered, for about 10 minutes more.
▶ In a small bowl, put the raisins and pour the vinegar over them. Set aside to soak for 15 minutes, then drain.

MAKES 4 SERVINGS

1 medium head cauliflower (about 1 pound)
2 tablespoons extra-virgin olive oil
Kosher salt and freshly ground black pepper
2 tablespoons curry powder
2 cups water
1½ cups quinoa, rinsed until water runs clear
½ cup raisins
¼ cup apple cider vinegar
1 cup fresh cilantro leaves

FOR THE BEET-TAHINI DRESSING:
1 medium red beet (about 3 ounces), peeled and diced
¼ cup freshly squeezed lemon juice (from 1 large lemon)
¼ cup extra-virgin olive oil
2 tablespoons tahini
2 teaspoons honey
1 teaspoon lemon zest
⅛ teaspoon kosher salt

▶ To make the dressing, in a blender, puree the beet, lemon juice, oil, tahini, honey, zest, and salt until well combined and smooth. If the mixture is too thick, you may need to add water. Start with 1 or 2 tablespoons, up to 4 at most.

▶ To compose the bowls, in each bowl, put 1 cup of quinoa and top with equal portions of cauliflower, raisins, and cilantro. Spoon equal portions of the beet-tahini dressing into each bowl and serve.

SESAME TUNA
with Carrot Ribbons and Avocado Cream

I spent my friend's fortieth birthday on a beach in Hawaii. On the last day we splurged on beach-side lunch. Thankfully, they delivered an absolutely sublime meal that I have since thought of often. Simply steamed rice was topped with soy- and sesame-soaked cubes of tuna, plenty of vegetables, toasted sesame seeds, and a velvety avocado sauce, making for a light but filling lunch. If you've never worked with raw fish before, don't fret! This dish is easy to create and does not require sushi-making skills. Make the avocado cream last, as it discolors quickly.

▶ In a small bowl, stir together the tuna, tamari, oil, ginger, and thinly sliced green onion. Set aside in the refrigerator until ready to use.

▶ To make the rice, in a large pot over high heat, bring the water to a boil. Add the rice, stirring once, and reduce the heat to medium low, keeping the rice at a medium boil. Do not cover the pot. After 30 minutes, taste a spoonful of rice to make sure it is cooked through and no longer al dente. Strain the rice, add the salt, and return the rice to the pot, setting it off the heat and covering it. This will continue steaming the rice slightly and helps keep it fluffy.

▶ Using a vegetable peeler, make long shavings of carrot and set aside.

▶ To make the avocado cream, in a blender, puree the avocado, water, miso, lemon juice, honey, and mustard until very smooth, about 30 seconds.

▶ To compose the bowls, put 1 cup of cooked rice in each bowl and top with equal portions of the tuna, carrot shavings, remaining baton-cut green onions, sesame seeds, and serrano. Dollop equal portions of avocado cream into each bowl, add a slice of lime for squeezing, and serve immediately.

MAKES 4 SERVINGS

12 ounces raw albacore or yellowfin tuna, cut into ½-inch chunks
1 tablespoon tamari
1 tablespoon sesame oil
1 teaspoon grated fresh ginger
3 green onions, 1 thinly sliced and 2 cut into thin batons, divided
5 cups water
2 cups brown rice, rinsed until water runs clear
½ teaspoon kosher salt
2 medium carrots, peeled

FOR THE AVOCADO CREAM:
1 medium to large avocado
½ cup water
1 tablespoon white miso
1 tablespoon freshly squeezed lemon juice
1 teaspoon honey
1 teaspoon Dijon mustard

2 tablespoons toasted sesame seeds, for garnish
1 red serrano chili pepper, thinly sliced, for garnish
1 lime, quartered, for garnish

GARLIC OIL FARRO, ROASTED SHIITAKE, AND PECORINO

This grain bowl is reminiscent of risotto, minus the cream. Farro is similar to barley in that it's a chewy whole grain and takes longer to cook—worth it for the extra fiber. Fragrant garlic oil is made on the side, while the cooked flesh is used as flavor. Topped with toothsome roasted mushrooms and thick shavings of pecorino, this is a simple bowl for a humble meal. If you'd prefer a creamier version, simply stir in a spoonful of nonfat sour cream or even plain yogurt once the grain is fully cooked.

- ▶ Preheat the oven to 350 degrees F.
- ▶ In medium pot over high heat, bring the water, farro, and salt to a boil. Once boiling, cover and reduce to a simmer and cook until the farro is tender, 50 to 60 minutes. (Farro is cooked when it no longer squeaks against your teeth but is still slightly chewy.) Drain off any remaining cooking water and set aside, covered, until ready to use.
- ▶ On a large baking sheet, put the mushrooms and 2 tablespoons of the oil, tossing to coat evenly. Season to taste with salt and pepper and put in the oven. In a very small baking pan, add the remaining ¼ cup oil and the garlic and put in the oven. Roast both for 30 minutes; the garlic will be cooked through and translucent and the oil will be intensely flavored. The mushrooms will be crispy on the edges and chewy. Remove both from the oven and set aside.
- ▶ To compose the bowls, put 1 cup of cooked grains in each bowl and spoon over some garlic oil, tossing to coat. Season to taste with salt and pepper. Add a pile of roasted mushrooms, a spoonful of garlic cloves, pecorino, and serve.

MAKES 4 SERVINGS

3 cups water
1½ cups farro
¼ teaspoon kosher salt, plus more for seasoning
1 pound shiitake mushrooms, torn into halves
2 tablespoons plus ¼ cup extra-virgin olive oil, divided
Freshly ground black pepper
4 cloves garlic, smashed, peeled, and roughly chopped
3 ounces shaved pecorino

GRAIN INSPIRATION

BARLEY My childhood favorite, barley is typically available either as a whole grain with the hull intact (hulless barley) or pearled with the outer germ rubbed and removed (a.k.a. hulled or pearled barley). Whole barley does better if you give it a soak before using, both because that speeds up what is certain to be a long cooking process and because it helps make nutrients more available to our digestive systems. Pearled barley has been refined—its outer bran buffed off and so it steams quickly. It's important to note that whole barley will not absorb liquid as pearled barley will, so you cannot use them interchangeably with the recipes here. Just make sure to adjust cooking time and water as needed.

BULGUR Easy to prepare, bulgur requires no real cooking. You only need to boil water and let it steep into the grain. Use steamed bulgur as a base for a healthy and light meal. Bulgur is the product of wheat berries that have been steamed and dried, then broken down to a coarse grain of varying size. It is a staple in Middle Eastern recipes, so I look to them for kitchen inspiration. Opt for bulgur over white rice or couscous for its higher nutritional qualities.

FARRO Farro is the rock star grain of the group. Little known outside of Italy, farro is just now being grown domestically by a small handful of family farms. Also known as emmer, farro was introduced stateside by restaurants and has since started to find its way to the kitchen of many home cooks. Farro is worth sourcing online or keeping an eye out for at the farmers' market. Farro is nutty and firm, like barley, but the grain is softer and more refined.

QUINOA A mild-flavored, protein-packed grain, quinoa is widely available and comes in various hues—red, white, and yellow. Quinoa's wonderful texture is due to its germ (the outer hull), which breaks from the seed. The germ remains as a ring of crunchy texture encasing the soft and tender seed. Quinoa is gluten-free, as it is not a member of the wheat family. We call it a "grain," but in fact, it is an herbaceous flowering plant.

HERBY PEAS AND CRISPY GREEN RICE

Here, rice is first steamed and then baked in the oven giving it a kaleidoscope of texture in every bite—chewy, crispy, soft—that is undeniably entrancing. Then the rice is tossed with a bevy of herbs, lime zest, and sweet snap peas, adding lightness to every bite. It's a delicious meal to make ahead and have ready for pack-and-go lunches, as the rice maintains the texture over time.

▶ To cook the rice, in a medium pot with a lid, put the rice and add enough water so the rice is covered by 1 inch of water, cover, and bring to a boil over high heat. Reduce the heat to a simmer and cook until the water is absorbed, 12 to 15 minutes. Remove the pot from the heat, uncover, and set aside for about 5 minutes.

▶ While rice is cooling, preheat the oven to 350 degrees F.

▶ On a baking sheet, put the cooked rice and drizzle evenly with 3 tablespoons of the oil. Do not stir it, as this will break the grain. Roast the rice for 5 minutes. Remove the pan and stir the rice, coating it more evenly with the oil, and return the pan to the oven. Roast for 10 minutes more and remove the pan, setting it aside to cool slightly, about 5 minutes.

▶ In a large bowl, add the currants, mint, parsley, cilantro, dill, snap peas, green onion, lime zest and juice, honey, salt, and the remaining 2 tablespoons oil. Once the rice has cooled slightly, add it to the bowl and toss until well combined. Season to taste with salt and pepper and serve.

MAKES 4 TO 6 SERVINGS

1 cup basmati rice or other white rice
5 tablespoons extra-virgin olive oil, divided
½ cup dried currants
¼ cup finely chopped fresh mint leaves
¼ cup finely chopped fresh parsley
¼ cup finely chopped fresh cilantro
¼ cup finely chopped fresh dill
3 ounces sugar snap peas (about 20 pods), very thinly sliced
1 green onion, very thinly sliced
Zest from 1 medium lime
2 tablespoons freshly squeezed lime juice
1 teaspoon honey
¼ teaspoon kosher salt, plus more for seasoning
Freshly ground black pepper

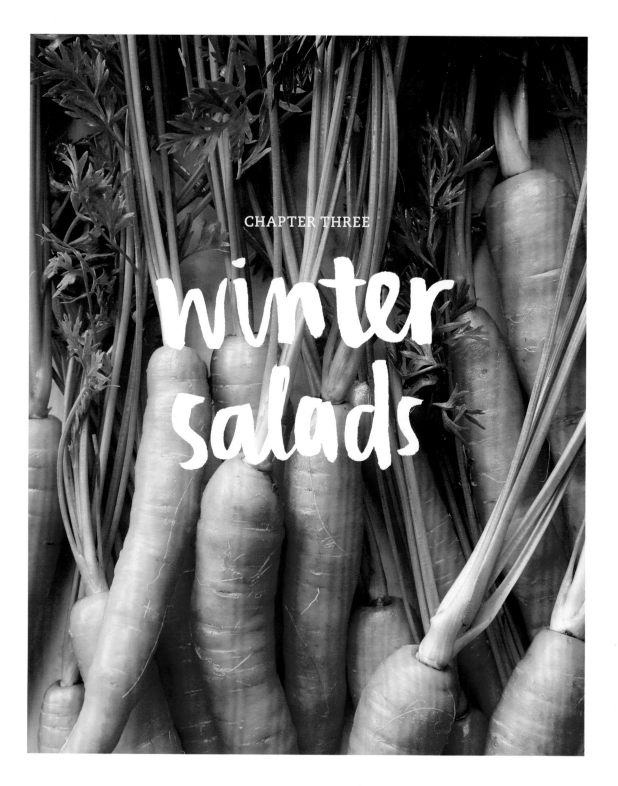

CHAPTER THREE

winter
salads

WINTER VEGETABLES ARE HARDY—gone are the days of delicate salads. A certain ingenuity is required with winter vegetable consumption—we can't always find the greens we are craving. Winter can feel like a barren season where lettuces are concerned, but there is a lot to choose from.

Strong-flavored chicories and avocados are plentiful, and there is a wide range of winter vegetables—kale, cabbages, apples, and more. Tough greens can be made palatable through fine knife skills, roasting, or macerating. A quick soak in some citrus juice helps soften leaves and adds flavor. And while greens aren't prolific in winter, citrus come into fruit during this time, offering a kaleidoscope of colors for the bowl. While it's habit to pick up a traditional orange from the shelves, branch out and source some other delicious fruits. Cara Cara, tangelos, Minneolas—each will offer a subtle change in flavor.

Packed with thick starches and winter stores, vegetables are satiating and can be made into meals on their own in winter. I will often whip together Root Vegetable Slaw with Salty Peanut Sauce (opposite page) for a midweek dinner. It's filling enough, thanks in part to the fat and protein found in peanut butter.

Flavors and textures vary widely from culture to culture, and varying spices alone will introduce new flavors to a standard winter vegetable. Swap out the herb used, or add a seasoned seed blend.

Go for a range of mouthfeels across your meals, mixing soft, crunchy, cooked, and raw. Ask yourself what you're going for in advance—do you want a small bit of apple or a big hunk? Do you want a mouthful of carrots (which take forever to chew) or just the flavor? You can shave vegetables; cut them into dice, matchsticks, rounds, or spears; or leave them whole.

Varying the cooking technique will also change a salad's texture. Baking produces soft flesh for most fruits and vegetables, while roasting at a high temperature allows natural sugars to caramelize and crisp. Dial up the heat and you get a dark char on food, offering a pungent flavor.

ROOT VEGETABLE SLAW
with Salty Peanut Sauce

This is my go-to salad in winter. The rich peanut dressing hits the spot every time and provides a nice bit of protein in an otherwise nutrient-rich, vegetable-packed salad. Be sure to cut the cabbage as thinly as possible—savoy is a nice frilly cabbage that is softer than a traditional head, but the thinner the slice, the gentler the salad is. If the cabbage is left too thick, you'll get a jaw workout, I promise! I like crunchy peanut butter in this salad, but use what you have.

▶ To make the peanut sauce, in a medium bowl, combine the peanut butter, water, soy sauce, vinegar, oil, fish sauce, and lime juice and smash with the tines of a fork until the peanut butter is well combined and the sauce is smooth. You can also puree the ingredients in a blender until smooth if you prefer, though if you're using crunchy peanut butter this will break down the pieces.

▶ In a large bowl, put the cabbage, carrots, beets, onions, and jalapeño and pour half of the peanut sauce over them. Stir until well combined and all the vegetables are evenly coated, adding more sauce as needed. Add the cilantro, stirring once, and serve immediately.

▶ Any leftovers hold well in the refrigerator up to 2 days. Leftover sauce will hold in the refrigerator about 2 weeks.

MAKES 4 SERVINGS

FOR THE PEANUT SAUCE:
½ cup crunchy or smooth
    peanut butter
¼ cup hot water
3 tablespoons soy sauce
2 tablespoons rice
    wine vinegar
1 tablespoon sesame oil
1 tablespoon fish sauce
Freshly squeezed juice from
    ½ large lime

½ medium head savoy
    cabbage, shredded
    (about 1 pound)
2 large carrots, peeled
    and grated
2 medium gold beets,
    peeled and grated
3 to 4 spring onions,
    chopped
1 medium jalapeño,
    thinly sliced
1 cup fresh cilantro leaves

ROASTED MOROCCAN CARROTS, CARROT-CUMIN YOGURT, HAZELNUTS, AND MINT
with Toasted Pita Crumbs

This salad is a textural Venn diagram of perfection—sweet, sour, creamy, crispy, spicy, and cooling intersect to create an intensely satisfying and gorgeous-looking salad. While it takes time to compose all the pieces, this dish is a showstopper, so it's worth the extra effort, especially if you're entertaining. The flavors embody the bold spices found in Middle Eastern cooking, a nice partner to sweet carrots. Carrots are both roasted and steamed here, making the most of this winter vegetable.

▸ Preheat the oven to 450 degrees F.
▸ On a large baking sheet, put the carrot sticks and toss with 2 tablespoons of the oil. Roast the carrots for 20 minutes, turning them once halfway through, until the carrots are dark brown at the edges and slightly crispy. Remove them from the oven and sprinkle with the salt, cayenne, and cinnamon, stirring to coat evenly. Set aside to cool.
▸ While the carrots are roasting, make the carrot-cumin yogurt. In a small saucepan over high heat, bring 1 inch of water to a boil and add the carrot rounds. Cover and steam until the carrots are very soft and tender, about 20 minutes. Remove the pan from the heat, drain completely, and let the carrots cool to room temperature. In a blender, blend the yogurt, cumin, and steamed carrots until completely smooth. Remove the yogurt from blender and chill in the refrigerator to set up, at least 20 minutes. (The yogurt can be made a day ahead.)

MAKES 4 SERVINGS

4 large carrots, peeled and cut into evenly sized sticks
4 tablespoons extra-virgin olive oil, divided
¼ teaspoon kosher salt, plus more for seasoning
¼ teaspoon ground cayenne pepper
⅛ teaspoon ground cinnamon

FOR THE CARROT-CUMIN YOGURT:
1 large carrot, peeled and cut into rounds
½ cup plain yogurt
¼ teaspoon ground cumin

½ cup toasted whole hazelnuts
5 cups pea vines or watercress
½ cup fresh mint leaves, torn (about 8 stalks)
1 tablespoon freshly squeezed lemon juice
Freshly ground black pepper
1 whole pita, toasted and ground into crumbs

▶ Remove the skins from the hazelnut by rubbing them in a dry linen cloth or paper towel. Place them on a cutting board, and using the flat of a large knife, smash the nuts into large pieces. Set the pieces aside.

▶ To compose the salad, on a large platter, set the pea vines and mint. Drizzle with the lemon juice and the remaining 2 tablespoons oil and stir to combine, being sure to coat all the greens evenly. Season to taste with salt and black pepper, stirring to combine. Across the platter, evenly dollop spoonfuls of the carrot-cumin yogurt, scatter the roasted carrots, and sprinkle the hazelnut pieces and pita crumbs. Serve immediately.

WINTER SALADS

ONION-POMEGRANATE SALAD

This wonderful make-ahead salad may intimidate some, as it deviates completely from a bowl of greens and uses onion as the main ingredient. It sounds odd, but it tastes great—the sweetness from the onions and the pomegranates complete each other, and in the bowl together, they make a pretty pairing. Feel free to add some orange segments for even more flavor. This salad is best served as an accompaniment to the main meal. Try making it alongside simply roasted meat or serving it over a bowl of curry.

▶ In a medium bowl, stir all the ingredients together and set aside to macerate for at least 20 minutes and up to 2 hours before serving.

MAKES 4 TO 6 SERVINGS

1 cup pomegranate seeds (from about ½ small pomegranate)
1 cup thinly sliced white onion or other sweet onion (about ½ onion)
¼ cup extra-virgin olive oil
2 tablespoons rice wine vinegar
2 teaspoons honey
⅛ teaspoon kosher salt

LEMONGRASS-PISTACHIO BRUSSELS SPROUTS AND LIME-SOAKED LEAVES

This salad is a mindblower. I had it at Nopi, a fancy restaurant in London, and from the first bite I was fascinated. Cooked and charred brussels sprouts are smothered in a fragrant, flavorful *sambal* of smashed herbs and spices, then tossed with fresh sprout leaves. The combination of both fresh and cooked brussels is lovely. If you can find the tops of a brussels sprout plant (check out the local farmers' market), use those leaves for the recipe—they are verdant and wider than the leaves on the actual sprout. You need a strong blender or food processor to break up the ingredients for this recipe. If you have an old machine, it's best to finely chop all the ingredients for the *sambal* first.

▶ Preheat the oven to 375 degrees F.
▶ To make the *sambal*, in a blender on high speed, puree the shallot, lemongrass, jalapeño, lime leaves, pistachio, coconut milk, ginger, garlic, and brown sugar. Through the feed tube on top, add the oil slowly until a paste is formed, about 1 minute. Scrape the *sambal* into a bowl and set aside until ready to use.
▶ Cut 1 pound of the brussels sprouts in half and put them on a large baking sheet. Drizzle with the oil and toss until evenly coated. Roast the brussels sprouts, stirring once halfway through, until the outer leaves are charred and burned, about 10 minutes. Remove the pan from oven and add 4 tablespoons of the *sambal*, tossing to coat evenly. Return the pan to oven and continue roasting until the *sambal* is charring, 7 to 10 minutes more.
▶ While the sprouts are roasting, peel the leaves off of the remaining ¼ pound brussels sprouts, being careful to leave them intact and whole. In a large

MAKES 4 SERVINGS

FOR THE *SAMBAL:*
½ medium shallot, roughly chopped
2 stalks lemongrass, outer layers removed and finely chopped
1 medium jalapeño, roughly chopped
3 makrut lime leaves
¼ cup whole pistachios
3 tablespoons coconut milk
2 tablespoons grated fresh ginger
1 clove garlic, peeled
1 teaspoon brown sugar
¼ cup extra-virgin olive oil

1¼ pounds brussels sprouts, divided
2 tablespoons extra-virgin olive oil
1 tablespoon freshly squeezed lime juice
Kosher salt and freshly ground black pepper
½ cup whole pistachios

bowl, put the leaves and lime juice, tossing until coated, and season to taste
with salt and pepper.

▶ Scrape the roasted brussels sprouts and bits of charred *sambal* into the bowl
with the fresh brussels sprout leaves. Add the remaining fresh *sambal* and the
pistachios to the bowl, stir to coat well, and serve.

CARROT, RADISH, AND TURNIP
with Garlic Bread Crumbs

Toasting bread crumbs adds a buttery bite to any meal and works particularly well with this root vegetable salad that is otherwise fresh and crisp. The magic in this salad is cutting the vegetables properly. Too wide a slice and you have a mouthful of peppery turnip where ultimately you should have a nice mix of everything on every forkful.

▶ In a large bowl, combine the vinegar, shallot, and mustard. Let the mixture sit for at least 10 minutes to help pickle the shallot and reduce the strong onion flavor. Add the carrots, turnips, radishes, and 3 tablespoons of the oil, stirring until well coated. Tear up one or two of the radish greens and add them to the bowl for color. Season to taste with salt and pepper and set aside.

▶ In a medium sauté pan over medium-high heat, heat the remaining 2 tablespoons oil. When the oil is hot, add the garlic, stirring constantly until it begins to toast, about 2 minutes. Stir in the bread crumbs. They will seem dry at first, but keep stirring and eventually they will turn glossy from absorbing the oil. Stir continually until the bread crumbs are golden brown and fragrant, 4 to 5 minutes. Remove them from the heat and set aside. To serve, place the salad in a large, shallow bowl and sprinkle the bread crumbs evenly over the top.

MAKES 4 SERVINGS

1 tablespoon apple cider vinegar
1 tablespoon minced shallot
½ teaspoon Dijon mustard
2 medium carrots, peeled and cut into thin matchsticks
2 white turnips, peeled and cut into thin matchsticks
1 bunch radishes, greens trimmed off and reserved, radishes cut into thin rounds
5 tablespoons extra-virgin olive oil, divided
Kosher salt and freshly ground black pepper
2 cloves garlic, minced
¼ cup dry, coarse bread crumbs

BROCCOLI "STEAKS"
with Zucchini Hummus and Curried Puffed Rice

Thick slices of broccoli are grilled, making the "steaks" in this recipe, and are set over a bed of pureed zucchini and tahini. My friend Michelle, a Paleo-eating nutritionist, offered up this idea for a filling vegan meal—she grills her broccoli on the barbecue, but using a griddle pan works just as well. The trick is using very high heat to maximize char and minimize mushiness—go for al dente. The zucchini hummus is rich with tahini and the curried rice puffs add needed crispness. This is a delightful dish for a light evening meal, and I highly recommend you make extra hummus for snacking.

▶ Preheat the broiler. On a large baking sheet, put the zucchini and garlic and drizzle with 2 tablespoons of the oil, tossing to coat evenly. Season to taste with salt and pepper and put under the broiler, on the highest rack position in the oven. Broil until the zucchini is browned and blistered, 4 to 5 minutes. Turn the zucchini over and broil the other side until browned, about 5 minutes more. Remove it from the oven and scrape the oil, zucchini, and garlic in a blender and cover, allowing the zucchini to soften and steam, for at least 15 minutes.

▶ While the zucchini is steaming, make the curried puffed rice. In a medium bowl, combine the paprika, nutmeg, turmeric, salt, cinnamon, and cayenne. Add the puffed rice and fold once or twice to coat with the spices. Drizzle the melted butter over the top of the rice and immediately fold, coating the puffed rice evenly. Set aside.

▶ After the zucchini has softened, add the tahini and lemon juice and zest to the blender and puree. With the machine running on high speed, drizzle in 2 tablespoons of the oil until well blended. Set aside.

MAKES 4 SERVINGS

1½ pounds zucchini (3 to 4 medium zucchinis), cut into 1-inch-thick slices, lengthwise
4 cloves garlic, smashed
6 tablespoons extra-virgin olive oil, divided
Kosher salt and freshly ground black pepper

FOR THE CURRIED PUFFED RICE:
½ teaspoon ground paprika
½ teaspoon freshly grated nutmeg
½ teaspoon ground turmeric
¼ teaspoon kosher salt
¼ teaspoon ground cinnamon
¼ teaspoon ground cayenne pepper
1 cup puffed rice
1 tablespoon unsalted butter, melted

1 tablespoon tahini
1 tablespoon freshly squeezed lemon juice
1 teaspoon lemon zest
1 large head of broccoli with a fat stalk, cut lengthwise into ½-inch-thick cross sections
¼ cup toasted pine nuts

- On a large baking sheet, place the broccoli steaks and drizzle them with the remaining 2 tablespoons oil, turning once or twice until both sides are coated. Season to taste with salt and pepper. Put a griddle pan on high heat and leave it for a few minutes, until smoking hot. Grill the broccoli in batches, charring both sides but being sure not to overcook. The broccoli steaks should be al dente, not mushy.
- To compose each plate, serve a heaping portion of zucchini hummus topped with one broccoli steak. Garnish with some puffed rice and a sprinkling of pine nuts and serve.

ROASTED CARROTS
with Sesame Tofu and Watercress

This salad is so delicious that I've actually eaten the entire recipe by myself more than once. It really is that tasty. Tofu is a vegan option for anyone conforming to a strictly plant-based diet, and as such is safe for use in the vinaigrette recipe. If you substitute meat instead, be sure to reserve some of the flavorful marinade before soaking the meat. Texture is added by crisping up the tofu and slicing the carrot into ribbons. They cook up chip-like and offer crisp to the plate.

▶ Preheat the oven to 425 degrees F.

▶ Press the tofu slices between a layer of paper towels, gently squeezing out most of the liquid, just until the tofu is damp. You may have to do this several times.

▶ In a small, shallow pan or on a baking sheet, combine the tamari, syrup, ginger, and cayenne. Lay the tofu slices in the marinade and set aside, turning occasionally, for at least 15 minutes and up to an hour.

▶ Using a vegetable peeler or mandoline, slice the carrots by making long, thin slices down the length of the root. On a large baking sheet, put the carrot ribbons and toss them with 3 tablespoons of the oil. Season to taste with salt and pepper. Roast the carrots until they are burned on the edges and have softened, 15 to 20 minutes, tossing every 5 minutes.

▶ While the carrots are roasting, sauté the tofu. In a large sauté pan over medium-high heat, heat 3 tablespoons of the oil. When the oil is hot (it will ripple on the surface), add the tofu slices and cook them until crisp and brown, 3 to 4 minutes. Turn them over and cook the other side until brown and crisp, 3 to 4 minutes more. Remove the tofu from the heat and set aside. Do not throw away the marinade.

▶ In a large bowl, put the watercress, carrot ribbons, the remaining 3 tablespoons oil, and 2 tablespoons of the marinade and toss until the greens are well coated. Divide the salad evenly across four plates. Arrange two pieces of tofu on each plate and sprinkle with sesame seeds before serving.

MAKES 4 SERVINGS

1 pack tofu (about 12 to 14 ounces) cut into 8 (1-inch-thick) slices
¼ cup tamari
1 tablespoon maple syrup
1 tablespoon grated fresh ginger
⅛ teaspoon ground cayenne pepper
4 large carrots, peeled
9 tablespoons extra-virgin olive oil, divided
Kosher salt and freshly ground black pepper
5 cups watercress
2 tablespoons toasted sesame seed

PANZANELLA KALE SALAD
with Lemon-Parmesan Dressing

Panzanella makes use of day-old bread, which helps reduce waste and bulk up salads. I prefer to grill or broil my bread cubes until they are almost burned. That black char gives the salad a nice flavor. Here, kale is cut into super-thin ribbons and left to sit in the vinaigrette for a bit, helping tenderize the tough, dark greens. Paired with a healthy shave of Parmesan (grate on a rasp to ensure delicate, feathery ribbons) and a pinch of red chili flakes, this dish makes a hearty salad course.

▶ In a large bowl, put the zest, vinegar, shallot, and anchovies and stir with a fork, breaking up the anchovies, until well combined. Set aside to let the shallots macerate for about 5 minutes. After the shallots have soaked, add the kale and toss to combine well (make sure all the kale is coated). Set aside for about 15 minutes more to allow the kale to break down slightly.

▶ Once the kale has softened, add the bread, oil, and chili flakes, and toss well until combined. Let the mixture sit for 10 minutes, and season to taste with salt and pepper. Add the Parmesan, toss to combine, and serve.

MAKES 4 SERVINGS

Zest of 1 medium lemon
2 tablespoons sherry vinegar
1 tablespoon finely chopped shallot
2 tinned anchovy fillets (optional)
1 bunch kale, stemmed and cut into ¼-inch-wide ribbons
4 cups day-old bread, cut into 1-inch cubes, brushed with extra-virgin olive oil, and grilled or broiled until charred ¼ cup extra-virgin olive oil, plus more for brushing
¼ teaspoon red chili flakes
Kosher salt and freshly ground black pepper
1 cup freshly grated Parmesan

ROASTED BEETS
with Pistachio and Creamy Horseradish-Dill Dressing

A quintessential winter salad, roasted beets are plentiful in colder months. This recipe has similar flavors to what you'd find in borscht—beets, dill, and yogurt are historically brilliant together. Crispness and nuttiness are added with the pistachio, in addition to a bright, green flavor that perks up your other senses. You can dial down the heat here by adding less horseradish to the dressing. Personally, I like it hot.

▸ Preheat the oven to 425 degrees F.
▸ Scrub the beets free of all dirt. In a shallow baking dish, put the beets, toss them with the oil, and season to taste with salt and pepper. Cover the baking sheet with aluminum foil and roast until the beets can be pierced through the center with a knife but are still firm, 50 to 60 minutes.
▸ While the beets are roasting, make the horseradish-dill dressing. In a small bowl, stir together the yogurt, oil, and horseradish until well blended.
▸ On a large platter, put the arugula and dill and toss to combine, then spread them out evenly on the platter. Set aside.
▸ Once the beets are cooked through, remove them from the oven and set them aside until they are cool enough to handle before rubbing off the skins with paper towels. Cut each beet into sixths and spread them evenly across the platter. Sprinkle the salad evenly with the pistachios and salt. Drizzle the dressing over the salad and serve.

MAKES 4 TO 6 SERVINGS

4 to 5 medium red beets
2 tablespoons extra-virgin olive oil
⅛ teaspoon kosher salt, plus more for seasoning
Freshly ground black pepper

FOR THE HORSERADISH-DILL DRESSING:
¼ cup plain yogurt
2 tablespoons extra-virgin olive oil
2 tablespoons grated fresh horseradish

4 cups arugula
¼ cup roughly chopped fresh dill
¼ cup whole pistachios

WILTED ROMAINE AND GINGER BEEF

I love cooking lettuce. While wilted lettuce in the bottom of a bowl is not appetizing, intentionally wilted lettuce can be a revelation. The flavors are often pronounced and they are very quick cooking! Here, ground beef is cooked in a ginger-and-garlic-spiked sauce that is lovely served over a bed of rice or other grain, though I prefer eating it as is. Of course, you can substitute the meat using ground turkey or even tofu. This warm salad is salty, hot, crunchy, gingery, and delicious—try it. (A note about the addition of cornstarch—using the cornstarch will thicken the sauce and help it coat the lettuce leaves. While I forgo this in my own kitchen, most people gravitate toward a thicker sauce, so it's added here. Feel free to skip it!)

MAKES 4 SERVINGS

6 cups romaine (1 medium head romaine, cut into 2-inch-wide strips)
1 tablespoon extra-virgin olive oil
1 tablespoon grated garlic
2 tablespoons grated fresh ginger
½ pound lean ground beef
½ cup water
¼ cup tamari
1 teaspoon cornstarch or all-purpose flour (optional)
1 jalapeño, sliced
1 cup fresh cilantro leaves

▶ In a large salad bowl, put the lettuce and set aside.
▶ In a deep-sided and large sauté pan over medium-high heat, heat the oil. When the oil is hot (the surface will ripple), add the garlic and stir continuously for 1 minute, making sure the garlic does not burn. After 1 minute, add the ginger and stir continuously for 2 minutes. The ginger juice will splatter, but don't be alarmed. The garlic should be starting to toast now, and the air will be fragrant. Add the beef and cook, stirring often and breaking into small pieces, until browned and cooked, about 7 minutes.
▶ Add the water, tamari, and cornstarch to the pan and turn the heat to high. Cook for 2 to 3 minutes, until the liquid is reduced and thickened slightly. To finish, pour the beef and sauce over the romaine and toss until the lettuce is well coated and slightly wilted. To serve, divide among shallow bowls and garnish with jalapeño and cilantro.

TO PEEL OR NOT TO PEEL

MANY VEGETABLES COME WITH AN EXTERIOR SKIN meant to protect the flesh from outside elements. Recipes will often call for peeling carrots, beets, or even broccoli stalks, but is it necessary to peel your veg?

Nutritionally speaking, leaving the peels intact maximizes your intake of good-for-you fiber. Vegetable skin cells contain strong plant cellulose, which is nutrient dense and high in beneficial vitamins. While there is a definite health benefit to consuming the skins, their flavor may be another story.

Root vegetables, in particular, are cultivated for a handful of attributes. Sweetness, days to maturation, storage capacity, and color vary across the spectrum of varieties available to growers, who choose certain seeds because of these specific traits. Some farmers may elect for a sweet, fresh-eating version instead of a vegetable that will store for long periods. These fresh-eating vegetables have a higher sugar content and are therefore more palatable. Because of their delicate skin, however, sweeter vegetables tend to have a shorter shelf life; they'll go limp and soft in a matter of days postharvest. Sweeter varieties work for farmers with easy access to market, but what if the farm is in the middle of nowhere?

Enter storage vegetables, which are grown for their ability to last, not their sweetness. Their thicker skin allows for a longer shelf life, which means they don't taste as fresh. The thicker the skin, the more bitter the flavor profile can range due to the tannins. As the vegetable ages and sugars in the plant naturally convert to carbohydrates, the flavor changes and becomes less sweet.

So, to peel or not to peel?

If you like the flavor with the peels on or you're using fresh-picked vegetables, why bother peeling? Just make sure you scrub dirt out of the skins before eating and wash vegetables under cool water first. Aesthetically, if you prefer a brightly colored vegetable (cooked carrot skins tend to turn gray and pale, which may not be appealing to some) or don't like the taste of a particular vegetable's peel, remove it.

CHAPTER FOUR

salads with fruit

FRUIT IN SALAD IS A POLARIZING THING, like ginger or cilantro—people tend to love it or hate it. I love it. Natural sugars found in all fruits complement vegetables and make for a well-rounded flavor profile in every bite.

Fruits can be left whole or sliced, cooked, dried, or smashed before being added to salads—all of which will provide a different texture, allowing for infinite possibilities. Don't limit yourself when thinking about how a fruit salad will come together. You've likely had a few apple slices in a salad before, but what about apple shavings? Try cutting them into matchsticks or even altering the slicing technique. This changes the texture of a simple salad and keeps things interesting.

Altering the fruit slightly will also introduce new flavors and textures to a salad. Use dehydrated fruits—raisins are a given, but how about a dehydrated apple instead? Dried fruits like dates and raisins are sweet-forward—they tend to linger on the palate and offer a super-sweet bite to meals. Dried plums, cherries, and other stone fruits as well as all dried berries introduce a tart-sweet flavor that does well with bitter greens or strong winter leaves. You can pickle fruit in vinegar before adding it to a salad—the acid punches up the flavor and provides a tangy-fruity bite.

FENNEL AND PLUMS
with Honey-Ginger Vinaigrette

The first time I made and tried this recipe, I ate the entire bowl. These flavor and texture combinations make for a perfect salad! Here, it's important to shave the fennel bulb—using a mandoline is a lifesaver, but if you don't have that, use a knife, go slow, and get it as thin as possible. If left too thick, fresh fennel is hard to chew and can taste too much like anise to some. Save any leftover vinaigrette for your next salad or even a marinade—this dressing is a keeper.

▶ To make the vinaigrette, in a large bowl, whisk the oil, vinegar, honey, ginger, salt, and pepper until well combined.
▶ Put the fennel and plum slices into the bowl and fold gently, until all are well coated. Let the salad sit for 10 minutes. Season to taste with salt and pepper and serve.

MAKES 4 SERVINGS

FOR THE HONEY-GINGER VINAIGRETTE:
3 tablespoons extra-virgin olive oil
1 tablespoon white wine vinegar
1 tablespoon honey
1 teaspoon grated fresh ginger
Kosher salt and freshly ground black pepper

1 medium fennel bulb (about ½ pound), cored and shaved thin
2 medium plums (about ½ pound), halved and thinly sliced

CHARRED ONION AND BALSAMIC CHERRIES
with Mustard Greens

This harmonious marriage of burned onion and fresh cherries is a summertime favorite of mine. I use this combo as a relish, as a condiment to grilled meat, and here, in a salad. Charred onions are crispy and delightful—their burned flesh mellows the bite of raw onion and brings out the savory quality in the best way. Here, hot onions macerate with fresh cherries, their warmth drawing out some juices, and make a lovely base for salad. I prefer the peppery bite from mustard greens like mizuna or ruby streaks, but feel free to use arugula or even a more delicate frisée, as it adds so much texture.

MAKES 4 SERVINGS

5 torpedo onions or other small, oval-shaped onions, cut into ½-inch slices
4 tablespoons extra-virgin olive oil, divided
2 cups Bing cherries, pitted and halved
1 teaspoon honey
1 teaspoon apple cider vinegar
½ teaspoon kosher salt, plus more for seasoning
4 cups mizuna or mustard green mix
Freshly ground black pepper

▶ Preheat the oven to 450 degrees F.
▶ On a large baking sheet, put the onions and toss with 3 tablespoons of the oil. Roast the onions until they are charred and the edges are blackening, turning them halfway through, about 20 minutes.
▶ While the onions are roasting, in a large bowl, put the cherries, honey, vinegar, and salt. Toss to combine and set aside.
▶ When the onions are done roasting, add them to the bowl, scraping all the oil from the baking sheet into the bowl. Cover the bowl with a plate or piece of plastic wrap and set it aside to cool, about 20 minutes.
▶ Once the cherry-onion mixture has cooled to warm, add the mizuna and the remaining 1 tablespoon oil to the bowl. Toss until well combined and season to taste with salt and pepper. Serve immediately.

BERRIES AND STONE FRUIT
with Lime–Poppy Seed Vinaigrette

I'm not a huge fan of fruit salads—the longer fruit sits in acid, the mushier the texture becomes. I prefer fruit laid out on a platter, not tossed into a big bowl, which keeps them fresh and whole. Be sure to use just-ripe produce for this salad and choose it for an occasion where the platter won't be sitting for hours. In winter, substitute bananas, mangoes, and kiwi. Any leftovers can be used to top morning granola bowls or added to a smoothie, as the creamy dressing is made from yogurt and fruit juice.

▸ Arrange the strawberries, raspberries, blueberries, peaches, and plums evenly across a large platter. Sprinkle the mint evenly on top.
▸ To make the vinaigrette, in a small jar, combine the yogurt, oil, poppy seeds, honey, and lime zest and juice and shake well for about 30 seconds. Drizzle the vinaigrette evenly over the fruit and serve immediately.

MAKES 4 SERVINGS

1 pint fresh strawberries, hulled and sliced
1 pint fresh raspberries
1 pint fresh blueberries
2 peaches, halved and then sliced
2 plums, halved and then sliced
½ cup fresh mint leaves, finely chopped

FOR THE LIME–POPPY SEED VINAIGRETTE:
2 tablespoons plain yogurt
2 tablespoons extra-virgin olive oil
2 tablespoons black poppy seeds
1 teaspoon honey
Zest from 1 medium lime
Freshly squeezed juice from 1 medium lime

SEASONS FOR FRUIT

AS THE SEASONS PASS BY, the type of fresh fruit offering will change, providing a revolving selection at any point in the year. Summer fruits are juicy all on their own, while in winter fresh citrus provides a bitter tang with only mild sweetness—excellent for waking up heavy winter meals. This calendar of fruits is an easy way to make informed choices at the grocery store—just choose what's in season and purchase that. Here's a short cheat sheet:

SEASONS FOR FRUIT:

NOVEMBER–MARCH Blood oranges, coconuts, grapefruit, kumquats, lemons, limes, mangoes, oranges, tropical fruits

APRIL–JUNE Blueberries, raspberries, rhubarb, strawberries

JULY–AUGUST All melons, apples, blackberries, cherries, figs, nectarines, peaches, plums

SEPTEMBER–OCTOBER All nuts, apples, cranberries, grapes, olives, pears, pumpkin, winter squash

FIGS AND ARUGULA
with Salami and Honey-Mustard Vinaigrette

This salad is the perfect recipe to let go of the pressure to use exact measurements and process. When I make it at home, I use a small spoon to grab ingredients for the vinaigrette and grab one heaping handful of greens per person—it's always delicious. On a recent summer visit, I spent a month in Croatia with my cousin and friends, and I made this salad every day simply because we had the ingredients around the house. My friend Matea brought a large, homemade sausage from her village, arugula was plentiful at the markets, and we always had figs on hand from the tree out back. The Croatians loved it—they wouldn't normally mix fruit into their salads, or add a hard sausage. A match made in heaven.

MAKES 4 SERVINGS

3 tablespoons extra-virgin olive oil
2 tablespoons apple cider vinegar
1 teaspoon Dijon mustard
1 teaspoon honey
4 cups arugula
4 ounces hard sausage, chopped
8 ripe figs, quartered
Kosher salt and freshly ground black pepper

▶ In a large bowl, whisk together the oil, vinegar, mustard, and honey until combined. Add the arugula, sausage, and figs and fold gently to combine. Season to taste with salt and pepper and serve.

SUMMER FRUITS
with Crushed Herbs

In this dish, fresh herbs are muddled to a thick paste and tossed with a handful of in-season fruits—tomatoes, peaches, and cantaloupe. Served at room temperature, this savory-sweet salad is pretty to look at and makes a wonderful side dish to grilled meats. Cut all the fruit into similar sizes so that you have a little bit of everything on every forkful. For a more fortifying salad, add a few spoonfuls of soft cheese like chèvre or ricotta to each serving.

▶ With a mortar and pestle, muddle the mint and cilantro by smashing them until they are broken down and juicy. Transfer the mixture to a large bowl, then add the cantaloupe, peach, tomatoes, salt, pepper, vinegar, and oil. Fold gently to combine, making sure everything is covered with the herbs. Set aside for the flavors to develop, about 10 minutes, before serving. Leftover salad can be held in the refrigerator, covered, for 1 day. Fresh herbs should be added to liven up the flavors before serving leftovers.

MAKES 4 SERVINGS

¼ cup fresh mint leaves
¼ cup fresh cilantro leaves
2 cups cubed cantaloupe
1 peach, cut into
   thin wedges
1 pound assorted tomatoes,
   larger tomatoes cut
   into wedges
¼ teaspoon kosher salt,
   plus more for seasoning
⅛ teaspoon freshly ground
   black pepper, plus more
   for seasoning
3 tablespoons apple
   cider vinegar
5 tablespoons extra-virgin
   olive oil

ORANGE AND PARSLEY
with Dried Olives

A surprisingly delicious salad, this makes the most of the few greens on offer in the dark of winter. Orange slices are covered in a thick mat of whole parsley leaves, while dry-cured olives offer a salty, toothsome edge. Easy to put together and made with super-affordable ingredients, this is a great salad to serve on a platter for crowds. If the oranges are a bit dry or sour, you can always drizzle a bit of honey over the tops as well. The orange flower water lends a subtle floral note, but you can omit it if it's not your thing.

MAKES 4 SERVINGS

4 large Navel or Cara Cara oranges, rinds and pith cut off, cut into thin rounds
½ bunch fresh parsley, leaves picked off and stems finely chopped
3 ounces dry-cured olives
¼ cup extra-virgin olive oil
1 tablespoon rice wine vinegar
⅛ teaspoon orange blossom water (optional)
Kosher salt and freshly ground black pepper

▶ To compose the salad, spread the orange slices in a single layer on a platter with the edges slightly overlapping. Sprinkle the parsley evenly across the oranges. Spread the olives evenly on top.

▶ In a small jar, combine the oil, vinegar, and orange blossom water. Shake vigorously until well combined and emulsified, about 30 seconds. Drizzle the vinaigrette evenly across the platter, season to taste with salt and pepper, and serve.

BUTTER LETTUCE
with Pink Grapefruit, Toasted Coconut, and Cayenne-Sesame Vinaigrette

This is a delicate and beautiful winter salad. Soft butter lettuce leaves fold around wedges of sweet pink grapefruit and rich avocado—a lovely pairing. Toasted coconut flakes offer both texture and flavor, while the cayenne-spiked vinaigrette has a bit of bite. All in all, it's as pretty as it is tasty—a great winter staple.

MAKES 4 SERVINGS

1 medium pink grapefruit
3 tablespoons avocado or
   extra-virgin olive oil
1 tablespoon apple
   cider vinegar
2 teaspoons honey
1/8 teaspoon ground
   cayenne pepper
1/8 teaspoon sesame oil
1 medium head
   butter lettuce
2 Belgian endives, cut into
   1-inch slices
1 medium avocado,
   thinly sliced
1 cup toasted coconut flakes

▶ To make the grapefruit supremes, cut both the top and bottom from the grapefruit and set it on a cutting board, cut side up. Using a sharp knife, carefully cut off the peel by running the knife lengthwise from top to bottom, removing only the peel and white pith. Be careful not to cut too deeply into the fruit flesh. Holding the fruit over a large bowl to catch the juices, slice segments between the membranes, working toward the center of the fruit. Rotate the grapefruit as you work, until all the flesh has been cut out into triangular segments. You should have about 1 cup of fruit. Squeeze any residual juice from the membranes into the bowl, about 2 or 3 tablespoons, and discard membranes.

▶ To the bowl with the grapefruit juice and supremes, add the avocado oil, vinegar, honey, cayenne, and sesame oil. Whisk until well combined and emulsified. Add the butter lettuce, endives, and avocado to the bowl and fold until well combined.

▶ Portion the salad equally across four plates. Over each salad, drizzle any remaining vinaigrette and scatter the coconut before serving.

CELERY AND CITRUS SALAD
with Chilies

Celery is a vegetable that many people keep lying in the crisper for weeks on end but seldom gets used or appreciated. Happily, celery can be a lifesaver for making salads—it's something green, it's crispy, and it's affordable. Here, we lean on the tender, light-colored interior heart to make a colorful and flavor-forward salad, leaves and all. Sliced thinly and paired with creamy avocado and tangy orange slices, this is the perfect salad for feeding a crowd and a great item to pack if you're traveling—the celery won't break down and turn to mush, and it is infinitely healthier than any food you'll find at an airport.

MAKES 4 SERVINGS

8 celery stalks from the heart or 4 large celery stalks
1 large Naval, Cara Cara, or Valencia orange
1 large avocado, cubed
2 tablespoons extra-virgin olive oil
1 tablespoon apple cider vinegar
½ teaspoon Dijon mustard
½ teaspoon honey
¼ teaspoon red chili flakes
Kosher salt and freshly ground black pepper

▶ Cut the celery stalks and leaves, working slowly to cut them as close to paper thin as possible. In a large bowl, put the sliced celery. (If using large stalks of celery, you can slice thinly on a mandoline.)

▶ To prepare the orange, cut both the top and bottom from the orange and set it on a cutting board, cut side up. Using a sharp knife, carefully cut off the peel by running the knife lengthwise from top to bottom, removing only the peel and white pith. Be careful not to cut too deeply into the fruit flesh. Hold the orange over the celery bowl to catch the juices, cut segments between the membranes, working toward the center for the fruit. Rotate the orange as you work, until all the flesh has been cut out into triangular segment. Add the orange wedges to the bowl. Squeeze any residual juice from the membranes into the bowl and discard the membranes.

▶ Add the avocado, oil, vinegar, mustard, honey, and chili flakes to the bowl and fold to combine well, making sure no lumps of mustard or honey are left. Season to taste with the salt and pepper and serve.

hearty bean salads

RICH IN PROTEIN AND HIGH IN FIBER, beans act as hearty sustenance offering a level of nutrition that not many other foods can. They are made up of mostly complex carbohydrates and are an excellent source of iron and protein. Legumes are considered a superfood—one that promotes health and aids in disease prevention.

Beans have been cultivated for centuries and are available in many varieties. They can be mealy with a chewy skin or thin-skinned and buttery, depending on the variety. There are broad beans, like favas and corona beans; smaller beans that cook up creamy, like cannellinis and soybeans; and then of course fast-cooking lentils, which come in several colors and textures.

I prefer dried beans over canned beans. Dried beans have better texture than canned beans that have been sitting in water (although in a pinch canned beans will work). I purchase my dried beans direct from the farmer, at local markets, or online at various farms across the country. Bulk bins are also a great resource for buying dried beans, just buy small amounts. Keep in mind that one cup of dried beans can serve four people.

While dried beans have a long shelf life and don't often suffer from spoilage, aged beans may take longer to cook. Dried beans do well with a soaking before cooking. Setting them out on the counter overnight gives them enough time to soften and helps break down the simple sugars in legumes that we cannot fully digest. After soaking, it is imperative to discard the soaking liquid and use fresh water for cooking. (Small legumes such as lentils do not need to soak, as they cook quickly.) That said, beans can be a maddening and perplexing ingredient in that sometimes they cook for an hour, and other days it will take four hours, depending on their age, storage, and more. Make sure to plan ahead and cook beans beforehand if you're pressed for time and don't commit yourself to the cooking times I suggest. It's quite possible your batch will cook faster or slower. You may also cook beans in a slow cooker or pressure cooker, which speeds up and eases the process.

In salads, the beans will hold for several days in the refrigerator, whereas the greens often will not. If you're cooking for two or avoiding leftovers entirely, cook all the beans, but halve the rest of the recipe, adding greens to order later or using the rest for another recipe entirely.

CELERY, CHICKPEA, AND RAISIN

This is one of my favorite salads ever. It's a great mix to pack for the plane or for box lunches, as the celery stands up to the vinaigrette and the flavors develop over time. The inner core of the celery bunch is soft and tender (the "heart"), but feel free to use the sturdier outer stalks as well—just make sure to slice them thin. Here, chickpeas are cooked from dried legumes, the most flavorful way to eat them, in my mind. You can of course shortcut with canned chickpeas, if you prefer. Creamy chickpeas, crisp celery, and sweet dried raisins are a wonderful medley. Try it. You will love it.

MAKES 4 TO 6 SERVINGS

1 cup dried chickpeas,
 soaked overnight
 and drained
Kosher salt
1 cup finely chopped celery
 heart, leaves removed
 and left whole
¼ cup golden raisins
¼ cup extra-virgin olive oil
2 tablespoons apple
 cider vinegar
1 tablespoon Dijon mustard
Freshly ground
 black pepper

▸ In a large stockpot, cover the chickpeas with 1½ inches of water, add enough salt so the water tastes mildly salty, and bring it to a boil over high heat. Reduce the heat to medium low and simmer until the beans are tender and creamy, 40 to 60 minutes. Drain and cool.

▸ In a large bowl, add the chickpeas, celery, raisins, oil, vinegar, and mustard and fold until well combined. Season to taste with salt and pepper and serve immediately. This salad can be made up to 2 hours ahead of time.

PICKLED CARROTS, HUMMUS, AND WARM DATES

This salad is a multistep process that can be made in advance and composed just before serving. The pickling spices are very typical in Indian cuisine and add an interesting fragrance. Romaine leaves add some green, pickled carrots have crunch and highly aromatic flavor, and the hummus is a healthy bit of protein. Leftovers can be stored in the refrigerator and used within two weeks. You can substitute canned chickpeas if you prefer not to wait for the cook time. Typically, my chickpeas take an hour, but it can be up to two or three depending on the age and storage of your dried beans.

MAKES 4 SERVINGS

1 cup dried chickpeas, soaked overnight and drained
Kosher salt
10 tablespoons extra-virgin olive oil, divided, plus more as needed
¼ teaspoon ground cumin
¼ teaspoon smoked paprika

FOR THE PICKLED CARROTS:
1 pound bulk carrots, cut into uniform matchsticks
¼ cup vegetable or grapeseed oil
½ teaspoon fenugreek seed
½ teaspoon black mustard seed
½ teaspoon fennel seed
½ teaspoon red chili flakes
½ teaspoon coriander seed
¼ teaspoon cumin seed
1 (1-inch) piece fresh ginger, peeled and finely diced (about 1 tablespoon)
1 clove garlic, roughly chopped
½ large yellow onion, thinly sliced
Kosher salt
2 cups apple cider vinegar
¾ cup sugar
1 (1-inch) piece lemon peel
1 (4-inch) cinnamon stick

1 tablespoon unsalted butter
8 whole dates, pitted and halved
8 whole leaves romaine, chopped

▶ In a large saucepan, cover the chickpeas with 1½ inches of water. Add a healthy pinch of salt and bring to a boil over high heat. Reduce the heat to medium low and simmer until tender, 40 to 60 minutes. Drain and put the chickpeas in a large bowl. Add 8 tablespoons of the olive oil, the cumin, and paprika and smash with the back of a fork until creamy and smooth. (Alternatively, add all the ingredients to a food processor and blend until well combined and smooth.) The hummus should be thick and have large pieces of chickpea along with smoother pieces—like chunky peanut butter. Add oil or water as needed to thin out to a consistency you prefer. Set aside until ready to use.

- To make the pickled carrots, in a medium bowl, put the carrot sticks and set aside. In a large sauté pan over medium-high heat, heat the oil until hot (the surface will ripple) . Stir in the fenugreek seed, black mustard seed, fennel seed, chili flakes, coriander seed, and cumin seed. When the spices begin to pop (about 4 minutes), add the ginger, garlic, onion, and a pinch of salt, stirring until they are soft and slightly caramelized, 6 to 8 minutes. Remove from the heat and add the vinegar, sugar, lemon peel, and cinnamon stick, stirring until all the sugar has dissolved. Pour the hot vinegar mixture over the carrots and set aside to pickle, at least until the brine is at room temperature, about 25 minutes. The pickled carrots can be made ahead and stored in a glass jar in the refrigerator for up to 2 weeks.
- To compose the salad, in a small sauté pan over medium-high heat, melt the butter. Once butter has melted, add the dates and stir until heated through, about 4 minutes. Remove the pan from the heat. In a small bowl, toss the romaine with 1 tablespoon of the pickle brine and the remaining 2 tablespoons oil.
- For individual platings, place a heaping spoonful of hummus on the plate and smear. Add a handful of carrot sticks and stack two dates on each plate. Place the romaine leaves on plate next to hummus and serve.

ROASTED BEETS AND KALE CRISPS
with Lentils and Tahini-Citrus Dressing

This is a great salad for winter time, as the flavors are robust and the salad is comfort food, like we all crave in winter, but healthy. Beets can be made in large batches so that you always have a few around to toss into salads. Here, they are paired with crisp kale leaves and flavorful lentils—just make sure you don't overcook the lentils lest they break apart into a bowl of mush. Drizzled with a rich tahini dressing, this salad is protein rich and delicious. While it has several components and is time-consuming, the steps to put this salad together are simple and worth it for an afternoon weekend or meal-planning menu.

▶ Preheat the oven to 425 degrees F.
▶ Scrub the beets free of all dirt. In a shallow baking dish, put the beets, toss them with 1 tablespoon of the oil, and season to taste with salt and pepper. Cover the baking dish with aluminum foil and roast until the beets can be pierced through the center with a knife but are still firm, 50 to 60 minutes. Once the beets are cooked through, remove them from the oven and let them cool slightly before rubbing off the skins with paper towels. Cut into sixths, season to taste with salt and pepper, and set aside.
▶ While the beets are roasting, in a large bowl, put the kale, 2 tablespoons of the oil, and the salt to taste. Using your hands, toss to combine well, so that all the pieces of kale are coated in oil. Massage the oil into the folds and crinkles of the kale and place on two baking sheets in a single layer (make sure the edges of the kale do not overlap); you may need to bake in batches. Put the baking sheets in the oven and roast until the kale is crispy but not charred, 15 to 20 minutes. Turn the kale chips over halfway through cooking to help dry

MAKES 4 SERVINGS

3 medium red beets
9 tablespoons extra-virgin olive oil, divided
1 teaspoon kosher salt, plus more for seasoning
Freshly ground black pepper
1 bunch kale, stemmed and torn into pieces
½ medium red onion, finely chopped
1 clove garlic, chopped
1 cup dried French lentils
2 tablespoons red wine vinegar
1 teaspoon Dijon mustard

FOR THE TAHINI DRESSING:
2 tablespoons tahini
1 teaspoon lemon zest
¼ cup freshly squeezed lemon juice (from 1 large lemon)
1 tablespoon grated fresh ginger
2 teaspoons honey
¼ cup extra-virgin olive oil
Kosher salt and freshly ground black pepper

them out. Small pieces will cook faster, so remove any pieces that crisp up early. Remove the baking sheets from the oven and set the kale chips aside to cool before serving.

▶ Cover the bottom of a medium saucepan with 2 tablespoons of the oil and heat over medium high. Add the onion and garlic and cook, stirring, for 5 to 7 minutes, or until soft. Add the lentils, salt, and enough water so that the lentils are just covered. Bring to a boil over high heat, reduce the heat to medium low, cover, and simmer until the lentils are cooked but are firm-tender, 20 to 25 minutes. Drain any excess water and pour the cooked lentils into a large bowl. Add the remaining 4 tablespoons oil, the vinegar, and mustard to the bowl and stir to combine well. Season to taste with salt and pepper and set aside.

▶ To make the tahini dressing, put the tahini, lemon zest and juice, ginger, honey, oil, and a pinch of the salt and pepper in a blender and puree until well combined and smooth. For a thinner consistency, add water. Start with 1 or 2 tablespoons and add 4 tablespoons at most. Season to taste with salt and pepper.

▶ To serve, pile dressed lentils onto a large plate or platter, scatter roasted beets evenly across the lentils, and then crumble over kale chips so they vary in size. Drizzle with tahini dressing and serve.

HEARTY BEAN SALADS

FRESH FAVAS
with Arugula Pesto

Fresh green fava beans are a real treat in spring, when the pods are picked and make a short appearance at the local markets. Like sweet peas, favas are juicy and have a meaty character that is satisfying. Drenched in a bath of arugula pesto, this salad is a verdant bowl with healthy proteins, fats, and fiber. If you can't find favas, feel free to substitute with fresh shelled English peas, or even frozen lima beans for a winter green fix. Don't use dried favas, as they lack the fresh green character that makes this salad so appealing, and prepare to spend a large bit of time peeling the fresh favas—it's a tedious task but worth it for the satiating quality of this large green bean.

**MAKES 4 MEAL OR
8 SIDE SERVINGS**

4 cups packed arugula
½ cup whole pistachios
1 tablespoon lemon zest
1 cup freshly grated
    Parmesan (about
    2 ounces)
½ cup good-quality extra-
    virgin olive oil, plus more
    as needed
Kosher salt
4 cups fresh fava beans
    (from about 2½ pounds
    fava pods)
Freshly ground
    black pepper

- ▶ In a food processor or strong blender, put the arugula, pistachios, lemon zest, Parmesan, and oil. Turn on the machine and process on high until all the ingredients are broken down and form a paste, about 30 seconds. If you'd like an oilier pesto, add another ½ cup of the oil. Otherwise, scrape the pesto into a large bowl and set aside.
- ▶ To prepare the fava beans, bring a large pot of water to a boil over high heat and season with salt. While the water is coming to a boil, prepare an ice water bath—add several ice cubes to a large bowl of cold water and set aside. Drop the fava beans into the boiling water and blanch for 1 minute, stirring occasionally. Drain the favas from the pot and plunge them into the ice water bath, allowing them to cool for 1 to 2 minutes. Peel the skin from the favas (it will come off easily after being blanched) or squeeze the skin until the bean pops out. (Some fava skins are thicker than others.)
- ▶ Add the warm fava beans to the pesto and stir to combine well. Season to taste with salt and pepper and serve.

CANNELLINIS AND BEETS
with Pickled Raisin and Radicchio

I was recently taking a class and this salad was easy to pack, hearty enough to sustain me through the afternoon, and light enough that I didn't grow sleepy. The sweetness from the beets and raisins really adds flavor, and there is a generous amount of vinaigrette for the beans to soak up. Topped with bitter radicchio and mild-flavored endive, this salad is a great go-to lunch dish.

▸ Preheat the oven to 425 degrees F.

▸ Scrub the beets free of all dirt. In a shallow baking dish, put the beets, toss them with 1 tablespoon of the oil, and season to taste with salt and pepper. Cover the baking dish with aluminum foil and roast until the beets can be pierced through the center with a knife but are still firm, 50 to 60 minutes. Once beets are cooked through, remove them from the oven and let them cool slightly before rubbing off the skins with paper towels. Cut each beet into sixths, season to taste with salt and pepper, and set aside.

▸ In a large stockpot over high heat, cover the beans with 1½ inches of water and add enough of the salt so the water tastes mildly salty. Bring to a boil, then reduce the heat to medium low, simmering until the beans are just tender, about 1 hour. Remove from the heat and set aside, covered, to steam the beans until soft and creamy, 15 to 30 minutes more. Check the texture of the beans every 10 minutes. (Be sure not to overcook and break them down.) When the beans are creamy and tender, drain any excess water and cool them slightly by spreading them on a large baking sheet in a single layer.

▸ In a small bowl, add the raisins and soak with the vinegar for at least 20 minutes, up to an hour.

▸ While the beans are cooling, in a large bowl, put the shallot, vinegar and raisins, honey, preserved lemon, and the remaining 5 tablespoons oil. Let the mixture sit for 10 minutes, curing the shallots. Stir in the beets and let it sit for 10 minutes more. Stir in the radicchio, endive, and beans. Season to taste with salt and pepper and serve.

MAKES 4 SERVINGS

3 medium red beets
6 tablespoons extra-virgin olive oil, divided
Kosher salt and freshly ground black pepper
2 cups dried cannellini beans, soaked overnight and drained
½ cup golden raisins
¼ cup apple cider vinegar
2 tablespoons minced shallot
1 teaspoon honey
1 tablespoon chopped preserved lemon or fresh lemon zest
2 cups chopped radicchio
1 Belgian endive, cut ½ inch wide

WHITE BEANS AND BLOOD ORANGES
with Spinach and Preserved Lemon

This salad offers beautiful colors to both the table and your diet! Ideally you want to cook the beans through without them falling apart. The trick is to pull the beans from the heat as soon as they are just cooked through and continue steaming them off the heat. Blood oranges add beautiful color and sweet acid to the mix—if you can't find blood oranges, choose Cara Caras or another orange-fleshed variety that you like. The vinaigrette here is deeply flavored with smoky spices and fresh herbs—a nice complement to a humble bowl of beans.

MAKES 4 TO 6 SERVINGS

1 cup dried white navy beans, soaked overnight and drained
Kosher salt
4 large blood oranges, rinds cut off and cut into ½-inch circular slices
¼ cup extra-virgin olive oil
¼ cup red wine vinegar
1 tablespoon Dijon mustard
1 tablespoon chopped preserved lemon
2 teaspoons chopped fresh mint leaves
2 teaspoons chopped fresh marjoram
1 clove garlic, minced
1 teaspoon ground smoked paprika
¼ teaspoon red chili flakes
½ pound spinach leaves
Freshly ground black pepper

▶ In a large stockpot, cover the navy beans with 1½ inches of water, add enough salt so the water tastes mildly salty, and bring to a boil over high heat. Reduce the heat to medium low and simmer until the beans are just tender, about 1 hour. Remove from the heat and set aside, covered, to steam the beans until soft and creamy, 15 to 30 minutes more. Check the texture of the beans every 10 minutes. (Be sure not to overcook and break them down.) When the beans are creamy and tender, drain any excess water and cool them slightly by spreading them on a large baking sheet in a single layer.

▶ While the beans are cooling, on a large plate or platter, arrange the orange slices so they are overlapping slightly and set aside.

▶ In a large bowl, whisk together the oil, vinegar, mustard, lemon, mint, marjoram, garlic, paprika, and chili flakes. Once the beans are slightly cooled but still warm, add them to the bowl with the vinaigrette and fold gently to coat. Add the spinach and stir until just dressed. Season to taste with salt and pepper.

▶ Gently pour the warm beans and spinach over the orange slices, spilling them in small piles so it looks pretty on the platter, and serve.

FRIED TURMERIC AND GINGER SOYBEANS
with Spinach

This salad is for health lovers everywhere who believe food is medicine. Turmeric root is becoming more widely available and it's a super ingredient both for its flavor and medicinal properties. An excellent anti-inflammatory, turmeric is also peppery, sharp, and earthy in flavor, adding punch and color to this salad. Gingerroot, too, is an excellent plant for its curative properties. It reduces swelling and helps settle the stomach. Both are strong-flavored roots, and this makes for a strongly flavored salad. Soybeans are creamy and small and packed with high-quality protein as well as being an excellent source of fiber. Throw in a few iron-rich, vitamin C–filled spinach leaves, and this salad is a perfect meal for hikes or a packed lunch for people looking to add more plant-based food to their diets.

MAKES 4 SERVINGS

2 cups dried soybeans, soaked overnight and drained
½ teaspoon kosher salt, plus more for seasoning
6 tablespoons extra-virgin olive oil, divided
1 medium to large shallot, peeled and thinly sliced
1 (6-inch) piece ginger, peeled and cut into matchsticks
1 (6-inch) piece turmeric, peeled and cut into matchsticks
6 tablespoons freshly squeezed orange juice (from 2 large oranges)
¼ cup apple cider vinegar
½ teaspoon freshly ground black pepper
4 cups spinach leaves

▶ In a large saucepan, put the soybeans and cover with 1½ inches of water. Add a healthy pinch of salt and bring to a boil over high heat. Reduce to a simmer and cook until tender, 60 to 90 minutes. (Check after an hour to see if they are soft!) Drain the soybeans and put them in a large bowl.

▶ In a large sauté pan over medium-high heat, add 3 tablespoons of the oil. Once the oil is rippling, add the shallot, ginger, and turmeric, stirring often and cooking until they are slightly browned and fragrant, 6 to 8 minutes. Add the orange juice to the pan, and immediately remove it from the heat, scraping up any burned bits. Add the vinegar, the remaining 3 tablespoons oil, the salt, and pepper to the pan.

▶ In the large bowl with the soybeans, put the spinach, add the warm vinaigrette, and gently fold to combine. Serve immediately.

noodle salads

THERE ARE TIMES WHEN I AM desperate for some vegetables and equally ravenous, and I know a simple green salad won't cut it. It's these moments when I turn to noodles. Noodles offer necessary carbohydrates and aid in the feeling of fullness. They also offer variety and texture to a salad and cook up quickly.

Many cultures rely on noodles for daily meals. Italians have pasta in hundreds of shapes and sizes, and in Asia noodles range from thick wheat udon to thread-thin rice noodles. Typically, I purchase a few of each and keep them stocked in my pantry, grabbing what inspires me in the moment or fulfills my dietary demands.

All noodles can be simply dressed and tossed with salad greens if you're crunched for time—just make sure to add more dressing. Here, the recipes reflect the extra bulk and the proportions on the dressings have been increased to make sure each noodle is generously coated.

Choose your green based on preference or texture. Fat noodles pair well with sturdy greens, whereas thin noodles partner with a spring green mix. Noodles also allow for expanding into other "salad green" territory with any vegetable. I cook down broccoli and carrots, mashing them into a salad sauce that coats and can be served at room temperature or chilled. Think of these as updated pasta salads. These are great for make-ahead meals or parties, as the flavor and texture will hold after hours of sitting in a bowl.

Cook times vary widely across noodle types, so always follow the package's directions. Wheat noodles are best if left slightly al dente, so be sure to taste regularly. Same with gluten-free pasta, if you're using that—a little undone is better than overly mushy pasta. Rice noodles are best if left in hot water until entirely soft. I like to salt my water every time I make a noodle, adding a bit of flavor, but you're welcome to skip this step.

Outside of traditional noodles, you can mix it up by using fresh noodles in any of the recipes. I suggest seaweed "noodles" in one of the recipes—they are made from kelp, are crisp, and are a brilliant choice for anyone with a dietary restriction.

PENNE SALAD
with Broccoli Garlic

Pasta salads are easy and filling—this is one of my favorites. A bountiful portion of garlic is slow cooked in an equally indulgent amount of olive oil, turning it velvety and sweet. From here, soft, steamed broccoli is added and smashed, breaking into small bits, before being combined with penne pasta. It's an excellent salad in summer, where it can sit in the heat for hours and not suffer—the flavor actually develops when slightly warm.

MAKES 4 TO 6 SERVINGS

2 large stalks broccoli
6 tablespoons extra-virgin olive oil, plus more as needed
6 cloves garlic, quartered
½ teaspoon kosher salt, plus more for seasoning
4 cups penne pasta
¼ teaspoon freshly ground black pepper, plus more for seasoning
½ cup freshly grated Parmesan or pecorino

▶ To prep the broccoli, cut off the stems along the main broccoli stalks, and break or cut off small pieces of the florets. Use a vegetable peeler to shave the outer, tough layer of the stalks, and finely chop the smaller stems and the peeled stalks. In a large saucepan over high heat, bring 2 cups of water to a boil. Add the broccoli florets, chopped stems, and stalks, and cover, reducing heat to medium low. Simmer until the broccoli is very soft and can be easily smashed with a fork, 25 to 30 minutes. Drain the broccoli and set aside.

▶ In a large, deep-sided sauté pan over medium heat, warm the oil, then add the garlic cloves and salt. Cook until the garlic is translucent and crisped on the outside, about 15 minutes. You do not want the cloves to brown, so reduce the heat if they are cooking too quickly.

▶ Meanwhile, bring a large pot of salted water to a boil over high heat and add the penne. Cook until al dente, about 12 minutes (or according to the instructions on the package). Drain, reserving ½ cup of the cooking liquid, and set aside.

▶ Add the steamed broccoli to the garlic and oil. Cook until the broccoli is very soft and starts to brown slightly, about 15 minutes, stirring occasionally, about once every 5 minutes. Using the back of a fork, smash the broccoli and garlic into small pieces. Add another spoonful of the oil if the pan goes dry.

▶ Increase the heat to high. When the broccoli starts sticking to the pan, stir in the reserved cooking liquid, cooked penne, and pepper. Remove the pan from the heat and serve immediately, portioning into shallow bowls, dividing the Parmesan evenly over the top of each serving, and seasoning to taste with salt and pepper.

BUCKWHEAT NOODLE AND STICKY SALMON
with Avocado-Miso Dressing

When I'm in a hurry, I quickly boil some soba noodles, which are traditionally made with buckwheat flour—a great gluten-free source of protein. (Buckwheat is a flower, not a grain.) Salmon, too, cooks very quickly and allows this meal to be on the table fast. Make the avocado-miso dressing last, as it discolors quickly.

▸ Prepare the soba noodles according to the instructions on the package. Drain well and put the noodles in a medium bowl. Set aside.

▸ To make the salmon, preheat the broiler. In a small bowl, combine the soy sauce and maple syrup and stir until combined and set aside. Rub the salmon fillets with the oil and season to taste with salt and pepper. On a parchment-lined baking sheet, place the fillets so they are not touching and put the baking sheet under the broiler and cook for 4 minutes. Remove the salmon from the oven and brush with half of the soy glaze. Put it back under the broiler for 1 minute more. Remove it from the oven again, glaze the salmon once more (using the rest of the glaze), and put it under the broiler again until the salmon is just cooked through and the glaze is blackening, 1 to 2 minutes. Remove the salmon from the oven and set aside.

▸ To make the avocado-miso dressing, in a blender on high speed, puree the avocado, water, miso, lemon juice, honey, and mustard until very smooth, about 30 seconds.

▸ In a medium bowl, toss the noodles with the avocado-miso dressing, spinach, cilantro, and mint until well combined. Divide the salad across four shallow bowls and top each with one piece of salmon and the green onions. Garnish with the sesame seeds and jalapeño and serve.

MAKES 4 SERVINGS

1 (8-ounce) package soba noodles
½ cup soy sauce
2 tablespoons maple syrup
4 (4-ounce) fillets wild salmon
2 tablespoons extra-virgin olive oil
Kosher salt and freshly ground black pepper

FOR THE AVOCADO-MISO DRESSING:
1 medium avocado
½ cup water
1 tablespoon white miso
1 tablespoon freshly squeezed lemon juice
1 teaspoon honey
1 teaspoon Dijon mustard

4 cups spinach leaves
½ cup fresh cilantro leaves
½ cup fresh mint leaves
2 green onions, chopped
2 tablespoons toasted sesame seeds (optional)
1 medium jalapeño, sliced (optional)

SESAME NOODLES
with Savoy Cabbage and Shredded Chicken

A traditional sesame noodle recipe, this salad is delicious served warm straight from the pan, or chilled in the refrigerator and eaten cold. They serve this dish at one of my favorite hole-in-the-wall Szechuan places in Seattle, and this is a close approximation, minus the hand-cut noodles. Noodles and frilly cabbage are tossed in a sesame dressing that is heavily spiked with red chili flakes—if you don't like heat, make sure to add less—and balances between spicy and cooling. Savoy cabbage is a frilly variety that is lighter and softer than traditional white cabbage, and chicken adds healthy, lean protein.

MAKES 4 SERVINGS

½ cup avocado oil
1 tablespoon red chili flakes
1 tablespoon sesame seeds
¼ cup tahini
¼ cup unseasoned rice vinegar
3 tablespoons soy sauce
2 teaspoons toasted sesame oil
1 teaspoon sugar
12 ounces ramen, udon, or soba noodles
3 cups shredded savoy cabbage
2 boneless, skinless chicken breasts (about 6 ounces each), poached and torn into large pieces
1 cup fresh cilantro leaves (optional)
1 cup bean sprouts (optional)

▶ In a large saucepan over medium-high heat, heat the avocado oil. When the oil begins to ripple slightly, add the chili flakes and sesame seeds and stir regularly until the seeds are toasted and fragrant. Add the tahini, vinegar, soy sauce, sesame oil, and sugar to the pan and remove from the heat. Whisk to combine until the sauce is smooth. Set aside.

▶ Cook the noodles according to the instructions on the package. Drain well, reserving ¼ cup of the cooking liquid, and put the noodles into the large sauté pan. Add some of the reserved cooking liquid to thin the sauce, if desired. Add the cabbage and chicken, and using large tongs, stir all to coat well.

▶ Divide warm salad among four bowls or plates and garnish with the cilantro and bean sprouts.

ARUGULA
with Carrot Pesto Orzo

I am a huge fan of cooked and mashed vegetables as a base for "pesto." This is a delicious room-temperature salad that can be made ahead or left to sit on a buffet table for hours without sacrificing the texture or flavor. This orzo pasta salad is a favorite for both adults and kids. The sweetness of the carrots appeal to all, and with a healthy dose of Parmesan over the top, it's a cheesy mass that most people adore.

MAKES 4 TO 6 SERVINGS

6 medium carrots (about 1 pound), peeled and halved lengthwise
6 tablespoons extra-virgin olive oil, divided, plus more for garnish
Kosher salt and freshly ground black pepper
½ cup toasted whole hazelnuts
½ cup freshly grated Parmesan or pecorino, plus more for garnish
1 clove garlic
1 pound orzo
6 cups arugula

▸ Preheat the oven to 475 degrees F.
▸ On a rimmed baking sheet, toss the carrots with 2 tablespoons of the oil and a pinch of the salt and pepper, until well coated. Spread the carrots out on the baking sheet so they are not touching, and roast for 20 minutes, until the carrots are cooked through and charred, turning once halfway through.
▸ Once the carrots are cooked, in a food processor or strong blender, put the carrots, hazelnuts, Parmesan, and garlic. With the food processor running slowly, pour in the remaining ¼ cup oil until well blended and pesto-like. Set aside until ready to use.
▸ Cook the orzo according to the instructions on the package. Drain, reserving ¼ cup of the cooking liquid. In a large bowl, combine the orzo, reserved cooking liquid, and carrot pesto. Stir well until the orzo is coated and the pesto is combined. Season to taste with salt and pepper. Fold in the arugula and serve. If you like, scoop the orzo onto a large platter and drizzle with additional oil and a sprinkling of Parmesan before serving.

TURMERIC GRILLED SHRIMP
with Rice Noodle, Nuac Cham, and Greens

This salad is friendly with all greens and it's a great way to use lettuce that needs eating. If you dine out and order a rice noodle bowl, its typically more noodles than greens, but here I inverse the portions making it a raw salad with a few noodles tossed in for texture. A traditional Vietnamese vinaigrette is used to liberally coat the veg, noodles, and shrimp—it's a generous portion of vinaigrette that you can use in one go or save some of for another recipe. Personally, I like mine soaked. Earthy flavor is added with the turmeric-coated shrimp—an appealing peppery bite that goes well with the cooling flavors of the salad, but be mindful as turmeric stains everything, clothes, countertops, pans, hands, etc.

- ▶ In a medium bowl, stir together the oil, turmeric, pepper, and a pinch of the salt until coated thickly. The marinade should be thick and paste-like. Add the shrimp, allowing them to marinate for at least 15 minutes, or you can leave them in the refrigerator overnight.
- ▶ To make the vinaigrette, in a medium bowl, combine the lime juice, fish sauce, brown sugar, water, and chili flakes, and stir until the brown sugar is dissolved. Set aside.
- ▶ To prepare the noodles, set a large saucepan of water over high heat and bring to a boil. While waiting for the water to boil, preheat the broiler. Once the water is boiling, remove the saucepan from the heat, drop in the rice noodles, and cook according to instructions on the package—about 5 minutes for most thin rice noodles—until just soft. Drain and rinse the noodles under cool water, which helps prevent them from sticking.
- ▶ In a large sauté pan over medium-high heat, add enough oil to coat the bottom of the pan in a pool of oil. When the oil is rippling, add the shrimp and cook until they're opaque on the sides, 2 to 3 minutes. (Don't panic if all the

MAKES 4 SERVINGS

2 tablespoons extra-virgin olive oil, plus more for cooking the shrimp
2 tablespoons ground turmeric
½ teaspoon freshly ground black pepper, plus more for seasoning
Kosher salt
1 pound shrimp or prawns, shelled and thawed

FOR THE VINAIGRETTE:
¾ cup freshly squeezed lime juice (from about 6 limes)
½ cup fish sauce
½ cup brown sugar
½ cup warm water
2 teaspoons red chili flakes

8 ounces rice noodles
8 cups mixed greens (spring greens, green leaf, romaine, watercress, etc.)
½ cup fresh mint leaves
½ cup fresh cilantro leaves

marinade does not stick to the shrimp.) Flip the shrimp over and cook until they are cooked through and firm, 2 to 3 minutes more. Remove the shrimp from the pan and set aside.

▶ To compose the salad, in a large bowl, put the greens, mint, cilantro, noodles, and half of the vinaigrette. Stir well to combine. Divide the salad evenly among four shallow bowls, top with equal portions of shrimp, and serve. Serve any extra vinaigrette on the side, and add as desired.

PASTA SALAD
with Sardines, Roasted Tomatoes, Pine Nuts, and Raisins

Sardines are full of omega-3 fatty acids (which have amazing anti-inflammatory properties), zinc, and calcium—they are an excellent fish to incorporate into your diet and are widely available and affordable as a tinned cold-water fish. Tomatoes are slow roasted, which concentrates their flavor into a sultry heap of chewy tomato. If you have room in the oven, make a double batch and save some for later. This salad can be made as a main meal, is great for crowds, and can be eaten hot, cold, or room temperature. While the ingredients are not the most common, don't shy away from this recipe. It's a winner.

MAKES 4 TO 6 SERVINGS

1 pound roma tomatoes or other paste variety, cut into ½-inch-thick slices
8 tablespoons extra-virgin olive oil, divided
Kosher salt and freshly ground black pepper
6 cloves garlic, smashed and roughly chopped
¼ cup pine nuts
2½ cups small pasta (penne, rigatoni, fusilli, farfalle)
¼ cup golden raisins
3 cups arugula
1 (4-ounce) tin sardines, drained and broken into large chunks

▸ Preheat the oven to 375 degrees F.
▸ On a baking sheet, spread the tomato slices in a single layer, being sure not to overlap the edges. Drizzle with 4 tablespoons of the oil and season to taste with salt and pepper. Bake for 45 minutes and then remove from the oven and turn the tomatoes over. Increase oven temperature to 400 degrees F and roast until the tomatoes have caramelized and are syrupy, about 20 minutes more.
▸ In a large sauté pan over medium-high heat, heat the remaining 4 tablespoons oil. Add the garlic and cook until softened, about 3 minutes. Add the pine nuts to pan and stir often until the nuts are toasted and brown, about 5 minutes more. Remove the pan from the heat. In a blender or food processor or with a mortar and pestle, puree the pine nut mixture into a chunky paste.
▸ To compose the salad, cook the pasta according to the instructions on the package. When cooked to al dente, drain the pasta, reserving ¼ cup of the cooking liquid, and add it to a large bowl. To the same bowl, add the reserved cooking liquid, roasted tomatoes, pine nut paste, and raisins, and fold to combine. Add the arugula and sardines and fold once or twice to combine. Season to taste with salt and pepper and serve.

SEAWEED NOODLE
with Shrimp and Peanut Sauce

Seaweed noodles are becoming more widely available at health food stores and co-ops, and it's worth a trip to source them. Made from kelp and sold raw, they are a nice change of pace from a starchy noodle, fresh and crispy, and a healthy, gluten-free option. Doused in a thick peanut sauce and tossed with steamed prawns and romaine, this is a great salad for a weekday lunch, as it keeps well and won't wilt or turn mushy once dressed. If you can't find seaweed noodles (either fresh or dry), substitute soba noodles or rice noodles—both will be equally delicious.

MAKES 4 SERVINGS

FOR THE PEANUT SAUCE:
½ cup crunchy or smooth
    peanut butter
¼ cup hot water
3 tablespoons soy sauce
2 tablespoons freshly
    squeezed lime juice
2 tablespoons rice
    wine vinegar
1 tablespoon sesame oil
1 tablespoon fish sauce

½ lemon, thinly sliced
1 tablespoon kosher salt
16 large shrimp, thawed
1 package seaweed noodle
    (about 12 ounces)
12 leaves romaine, cut into
    2-inch-wide ribbons

▶ To make the peanut sauce, in a medium bowl, combine the peanut butter, water, soy sauce, lime juice, vinegar, oil, and fish sauce, and smash together with the tines of a fork until the peanut butter is well combined and the sauce is smooth. You can also puree the ingredients in a blender on high speed if you prefer, though if you're using crunchy peanut butter, this will break down the nut pieces. Set the peanut sauce aside.

▶ To prepare the shrimp, fill a medium saucepan with water and set over high heat. Add the lemon slices and salt and bring to a boil. While the water is coming to a boil, prepare an ice water bath—add several ice cubes to a large bowl of cold water and set aside.

▶ Once the water in the saucepan is boiling, add the shrimp and cook until just cooked through, about 2 minutes. Do not overcook! Using a slotted spoon, remove the shrimp and immediately put them in the ice water bath to halt cooking. Once they are cool enough to handle, peel and set aside.

▶ While the shrimp are cooling, prepare the seaweed noodles according to the instructions on the package and transfer them to a large bowl. Add the romaine and pour over the peanut sauce. Stir well to combine. Portion the salad across four shallow bowls, top with equal servings of the shrimp, and serve.

CHAPTER SEVEN

fast & fresh
salads

In a pinch, a simple bowl of dressed greens makes for an easy vegetable choice at mealtime. In a sea of complicated salads with multiple steps, turning to a tossed salad for a quick bite to eat shouldn't be overlooked. At home my salads are typically thrown together in this fashion, and I will vary the vinaigrette or the greens to keep it interesting.

For a daily green salad the strategy is simple—purchase a bag of mixed lettuce or grab a head or two of leafy greens. Don't spend too much time thinking about what salad you'll make. Instead, let the greens on hand determine what to put together. Lighter greens like butter lettuce and baby spring greens go better with a lighter vinaigrette. Toothsome greens like kale, arugula, and mustard greens do well with a high-acid vinaigrette or thicker dressing—both of which help break down the greens and add flavor to these strong leaves.

Typically, I purchase two or three lettuces or mixed bags of greens, choosing what variety to grab by altering the flavor, color, and texture among them. My go-tos are arugula for its peppery bite; butter lettuce for its delicate flavor and soft mouthfeel; and a head of romaine or iceberg for its thick, watery rib and crispy nature. Whole, fresh herbs are also important—parsley, cilantro, and mint are the holy trinity of herbs that I always have in the crisper.

Within the recipes, feel free to sub out one chicory for another, or one tender green for a different option. I highly recommend that you continue mixing and matching across the families, which works to keep both your palate and visual system engaged.

Homemade vinaigrette can be as simple as a squeeze of citrus and some oil and salt, and that's what I've done here—kept it super simple. If you have an extra five minutes, opt for a more complex vinaigrette. If you truly only have thirty seconds, squeeze some lemon juice on your greens and be done with it.

MIXED GREENS
with Lemon Vinaigrette and Parmesan

This is an easy everyday salad recipe that I use as my primary vinaigrette when I don't have time or energy to emulsify, whisk, or wait for alliums to pickle quickly in an acid. Fresh lemon juice is a bright flavor and is simply squeezed over the top of the greens. Don't bother with measuring; just give a good squeeze and call it done—you can always adjust the next time you make it. To grow from here, swap out the acid (use a different vinegar every time) or the greens, and you'll never tire of making the same old thing.

MAKES 4 SERVINGS

6 cups mixed salad greens, torn into 3-inch pieces
½ lemon
3 tablespoons extra-virgin olive oil
Kosher salt and freshly ground black pepper
2 ounces shaved Parmesan

▶ In a large bowl, put the salad greens. Squeeze the lemon over the greens, pour the oil over, and toss to combine. Season to taste with salt and pepper, add the Parmesan, and serve.

CRISP ICEBERG, RADISH, AND CREAMY POPPY SEED DRESSING

Iceberg has a bit of a bad rap—this watery, crisp head of lettuce has suffered years of abuse as cheap lettuce green and a bad salad option. In actuality, iceberg lettuces are wonderfully crisp and full of water. When I want a lot of texture and a light, enjoyable salad, I'll grab iceberg. (It's good to note that homegrown iceberg lettuces are an entirely different beast than commercial heads, so if you have the space and inclination to do so, grow your own!) Here, the fresh leaves are paired with a creamy dressing and some peppery radish slivers. It's an easy salad for a weeknight dinner, the flavors are simple, and it makes for an elegant platter if leaves are left whole and stacked.

▸ To make the dressing, in a small bowl, add the yogurt, orange juice, oil, vinegar, poppy seeds, and zest and stir well until combined. Season to taste with salt and pepper and set aside until ready to use.

▸ Using a knife or mandoline, cut the radishes into paper-thin slivers. In a large bowl, combine the iceberg, reserved radish tops, and radish slivers. Pour the dressing over and toss until well coated. Serve immediately.

MAKES 4 SERVINGS

FOR THE POPPY SEED DRESSING:
¼ cup plain yogurt
¼ cup freshly squeezed orange juice (from 2 large oranges)
4 teaspoons extra-virgin olive oil
1 tablespoon apple cider vinegar
1 tablespoon black poppy seeds
2 teaspoons orange zest
Kosher salt and freshly ground black pepper

1 bunch radishes, leaves and stems removed, a handful of leaves reserved
1 medium head iceberg, chopped

GREEN ONION VINAIGRETTE
with Mixed Greens and Kale

I made this salad recently for friends, grabbing whatever greens they had in the refrigerator and any sort of onion I could use for flavoring the vinaigrette. The result was a toothsome, hearty salad that was big on flavor and came together fast. While most recipes would have you chop and garnish with green onions, here I pickle them in the vinegar first, which helps mellow out that oniony bite. If you happen to have the grill on, this vinaigrette becomes a little smoky when you grill the green onions first—try it both ways and see what you prefer.

MAKES 4 SERVINGS

3 green onions, roots removed and roughly chopped
2 tablespoons apple cider vinegar
1 teaspoon whole grain mustard
5 tablespoons extra-virgin olive oil
1 cup torn kale leaves
3 cups mixed spring greens
Kosher salt and freshly ground black pepper

▶ In a large bowl, stir together the onions, vinegar, and mustard until well combined. Let sit for 10 minutes.

▶ To the bowl, add the oil and whisk until well blended and emulsified. Add the kale and spring greens and toss to combine. Season to taste with salt and pepper and serve.

RADICCHIO AND ENDIVE
with Pickled Grapes and Soft Goat Cheese

Radicchio is bitter and often paired with another green, which mellows out the flavor, but here it takes center stage as the star of the salad. Bitter foods aid in digestion and don't break down as quickly as tender greens in the refrigerator, so they are easy to keep on hand. The radicchio's bitterness is counteracted here by a handful of sweet-pickled grapes, toasty pumpkin seed oil, and smooth, creamy goat cheese. Choose seedless grapes so you're not stuck biting into grape seeds midchew—not tasty. Make the grape pickles in advance if you'll be pressed for time, then store extra grapes in the refrigerator where they will keep for a few weeks. They make a great pairing with cheese plates and grilled meats.

MAKES 4 SERVINGS

2 cups purple seedless grapes
1 cup apple cider vinegar
½ cup sugar
10 whole cloves
2 Belgian endive, cut into 1-inch ribbons
½ large head radicchio, chopped (about 3 cups)
¼ cup pumpkin seed oil
Kosher salt and freshly ground black pepper
4 ounces chèvre, slightly crumbled into hunks

▶ In a medium bowl, put the grapes and set aside.
▶ In a small saucepan over high heat, bring the vinegar, sugar, and cloves to a boil. Reduce the heat to low and stir to dissolve the sugar, 2 to 3 minutes. Remove the pan from the heat and pour the vinegar mixture over grapes. Set aside until the brine and grapes are at room temperature or only slightly warm, about 20 minutes.
▶ Strain the grapes from the brine, picking out the cloves and reserving the brine, and put the grapes in a large salad bowl. Add the endive, radicchio, oil, and 2 tablespoons of the reserved pickling brine, and stir to combine. Season to taste with salt and pepper and fold before adding the chèvre. Fold the salad only once to combine without breaking down the chèvre, and serve.

HOW TO CHOOSE THE BEST LEAF FOR YOUR SALADS

THERE ARE MANY OPTIONS FOR ADDING greens to your salads, and while some greens are best for some recipes, it really boils down to what you prefer. Generally speaking, lettuces fall under several categories defined by their type and growing disposition. I've outlined them below as a quick shopping reference.

Unfortunately there is no real governing body for naming lettuces, and stores, farmers, and sellers all call the same species by different names, further confusing the customer. Buy what you like by tasting a small piece of the lettuce, and don't worry so much about what they're calling it. Further, I highly encourage you to grow your own lettuce greens. Anyone with a sunny balcony can grow all the lettuce they like with a shallow, long pot. Homegrown lettuces are incomparably flavored and allow for more variety. If you don't have space, time, or green thumbs, shop at your local farmers' market. They will always have a larger, fresher, and tastier selection than any store you find yourself in.

BUTTER LETTUCE We often see this sold as Bibb, butterhead, or Boston lettuce. The leaves of this variety (and there are likely more) are soft and buttery, hence the name. Often found in a protective plastic clamshell, these lettuces are hydroponically grown year-round, though if you find them at your farmers' markets, buy them there. The leaves from an outdoor growth cycle will be stronger in flavor, darker, more densely packed, and contain more nutrients.

LOOSELEAF A mix of lettuces, looseleafs are also called spring greens, and they're composed of any assortment of baby-size leaves that will often include a little bit from every salad family. Spring mixes are tender and delicate in taste, and they often include the oakleaf species of lettuces—named for their shape.

MUSTARDS AND BRASSICAS All dark green and toothsome, the brassica family includes broccoli and cauliflower and is known for its strong leaf varieties. They tend to be more popular in winter, as they are cold season crops, and many force you to chew, chew, chew to break down the fibrous leaves. They are also known for their spicy quality. Arugula, kale, turnip tops, radish tops, mustard spinach, ruby streaks, mizuna, and more are all brassicas.

CHICORIES These bitter lettuce greens do well in cooler climates and taste best during the shoulder season between winter and spring. Chicories sold in summer tend to be super bitter and can be off-putting. Radicchio, endive, escarole, frisée, and dandelion are all chicories. Often you will see them at the farmers' market or grocery store.

ROMAINES Romaine lettuces are the common salad green everyone knows. Used in a traditional Caesar salad, all greens in the romaine family have a thick, watery rib and tend to hold their crispness. Green leaf and red leaf lettuce you find at the grocery store are more often than not in the romaine family. Batavian is a subcategory within romaines, wherein a romaine and iceberg lettuce are crossed.

ICEBERG Icebergs are also known as crispheads, and while some people snub these densely packed white heads of salad, a head of homegrown iceberg lettuce is a thing of delicious beauty. Composed mostly of water, they are fresh and crisp. Please try growing some!

MUSTARD GREENS AND MAPLE-MUSTARD VINAIGRETTE
with Candied Pecans

Superior to spinach in terms of nutrients, mustard greens are often overlooked because they are thick and bitter. This salad, however, will sway you into their camp for life. Spicy greens are tossed in a sultry vinaigrette that is simultaneously sweet and pungent. Quick candied pecans add sweetness and smoky spice. This salad is a winning combination absolutely packed with flavor, though it comes together quickly.

▶ In a large glass bowl, stir together 2 tablespoons of the sugar, the cinnamon, cayenne, turmeric, paprika, nutmeg, and salt. Set aside.

▶ To make the candied pecans, cover the bottom of a large, deep-sided sauté pan with the peanut oil; let it pool a bit. Heat the pan over medium-high heat, and when the oil is beginning to ripple slightly, add the pecans, stirring continuously so they don't burn. When the pecans start to smoke and brown, add the remaining 4 tablespoons sugar and toss, toss, toss! You don't want to burn that sugar.

▶ After the sugar is dissolved and the nuts are well coated, use a slotted spoon to put the nuts in the sugar-spice mixture. Working quickly, stir to combine and then set aside to cool.

▶ In a large bowl, put the olive oil, mustard, syrup, and vinegar and stir briskly until well combined and thick. Add the greens and toss until well combined. Season to taste with salt and pepper, portion the salad out onto plates, and top with a handful of candied pecans.

MAKES 4 TO 6 SERVINGS

6 tablespoons sugar, divided
1 teaspoon ground cinnamon
1 teaspoon ground cayenne pepper
1 teaspoon ground turmeric
1 teaspoon ground paprika
1 teaspoon freshly grated nutmeg
1 teaspoon kosher salt, plus more for seasoning
¼ cup peanut oil
1 cup shelled pecans
5 tablespoons extra-virgin olive oil
1 tablespoon Dijon mustard
1 tablespoon maple syrup
1 tablespoon apple cider vinegar
6 cups mixed mustard greens (turnip tops, radish tops, arugula, mizuna, etc.)
Freshly ground black pepper

BUTTER LETTUCE
with Strawberry-Fennel Vinaigrette

Instead of simply being tossed into a salad, here strawberries are mashed to make a thick dressing that coats the greens, using a muddler. If you don't have a mortar and pestle, use the flat of a rolling pin or smash with a citrus reamer or even blend in a blender, if that's all you have. Adding smashed spices amps up the flavor too. Here, I use fennel for its cooling, digestive benefit, but you can use coriander seeds or any spice you prefer, or of course skip it entirely. You can add herbs, use raspberries instead, toss in some blue cheese, etc. It's a salad that can go in many directions or be enjoyed just as is—a fast and flavorful salad.

MAKES 4 SERVINGS

1 tablespoon fennel seeds
½ cup chopped fresh strawberries
2 tablespoons apple cider vinegar
¼ cup extra-virgin olive oil
1 medium head butter lettuce (about ½ pound), leaves separated from core and torn into roughly 3-inch pieces
2 large kale leaves, torn into 3-inch pieces
Kosher salt and freshly ground black pepper

▶ Using a mortar and pestle, crush the fennel seeds until they are broken down into coarse pieces. In a small bowl, muddle the strawberries until well broken down and juicy. It's okay if fleshy bits remain, but you don't want any large chunks. Add the crushed fennel seeds and the vinegar and stir well to combine.

▶ Pour the mixture into a glass jar, add the oil, and screw on the top. To emulsify, shake the jar vigorously for 1 to 2 minutes. When the vinaigrette is thick and creamy looking, set it aside until ready to use.

▶ To make the salad, in a large bowl, put the lettuce and kale leaves, pour the vinaigrette over them, and toss well to combine. Season to taste with salt and pepper and serve.

WHOLE ROMAINE
with Creamy Sumac Dressing

A spin on Caesar salad, the creamy dressing used here comes together faster and doesn't require raw eggs. Kids also love the creamy-cheesy dressing, so it's a decent recipe for getting the little ones interested in salads. For adults, I like to leave the romaine leaves whole and long, coating them in the dressing and then stacking them for a thoughtful presentation on the plate, though you can chop them if you prefer. Sumac is a Middle Eastern spice made from the bark of a bush and it has an appealing fruity, astringent flavor.

▶ To make the dressing, in a large, deep bowl, stir together the yogurt, Parmesan, oil, vinegar, honey, and sumac until combined. Season to taste with salt and pepper and adjust the acid and sweetness to your liking, adding more vinegar or honey as desired. To the bowl, add the romaine and use your hands to toss and coat well.

▶ To serve, stack four leaves on top of each other, crisscrossing them on the plate, and serve.

MAKES 4 SERVINGS

FOR THE SUMAC DRESSING:
¼ cup plain yogurt
3 tablespoons freshly grated Parmesan
2 tablespoons extra-virgin olive oil
2 tablespoons apple cider vinegar
1 teaspoon honey
1 teaspoon sumac
Kosher salt and freshly ground pepper

16 romaine leaves, left whole

STORAGE

MOST PRODUCE DOES BETTER WITH a little moisture and some air circulation. The crispers in refrigerators tend to do a good job of keeping moisture in, but to extend the life of produce, remove it from the produce bags. Fresh greens can be wrapped in single layers of slightly dampened linen towels. Apples can be kept in paper bags (although they do very well individually wrapped in tissue paper and stored in the garage), and herbs can be kept as you would fresh flowers—in small jars with an inch or so of water that is refreshed every other day. Most other vegetables should either be stored in the crisper on their own or wrapped loosely with a dish towel.

CRUSHED ALMONDS AND DANDELION GREENS

Dandelion greens are high in iron and packed with beneficial nutrients and antioxidants. They range from delicate to incredibly bitter—I always tear a small piece of leaf off at the store before buying. Bitter is okay with this recipe, though, as the greens are slathered in a coating of crushed almond and garlic—a hearty dressing for a very hearty green. Better served as a side salad, these greens can stand up to roasted and grilled meats and fish, making for an excellent-tasting and healthy accompaniment.

MAKES 4 SERVINGS

1 clove garlic, peeled
1 cup sliced almonds
1 bunch dandelion greens, divided
Zest from 1 medium lemon
1 teaspoon freshly squeezed lemon juice
3 tablespoons extra-virgin olive oil
Kosher salt and freshly ground black pepper

▶ Using a mortar and pestle, mash and grind the garlic clove. When the oils have covered the walls of the mortar, remove and discard the big pieces of garlic flesh. Add the almonds to the mortar and grind until they are broken up into smaller pieces. Add as many of the dandelion greens as you can fit (but no more than half), along with the zest, and mash all the ingredients together until combined. Work in batches if necessary. The mixture will look a little bit like a salad and a little bit like a pesto. Inconsistency in the size of the leafy bits is perfect.

▶ In a large bowl, put the remaining dandelion greens, tearing them into wide ribbons, and add the lemon juice, oil, and a pinch of salt. Give the greens a stir and add the smashed greens and almond mixture, stirring well until all the greens are coated. Season to taste with salt and pepper and serve.

SMOKED SALMON
with Citrus Vinaigrette

Smoked fish is a perfect kitchen staple to keep handy for fast, nutritious meals. It keeps in the refrigerator for weeks and the smoky flavor permeates recipes. Here, big hunks of salmon are added to salad greens and doused in a super-flavorful vinaigrette made from a rainbow of citrus juices and zest. The zing from the citrus cuts through the fatty smoke on the salmon and the greens add crispness and lightness. This is an excellent dinner to eat after an evening work out—it comes together fast, is nutritionally balanced, and is delicious.

▶ In a large bowl, put the citrus juices and zest, syrup, and oil. Whisk vigorously until well combined and emulsified.
▶ Add the romaine and avocado, tossing until the salad is coated. Evenly portion out the salad, top with equal amounts of the salmon, and serve.

MAKES 4 SERVINGS

4 tablespoons freshly squeezed orange juice
2 tablespoons freshly squeezed lime juice
2 tablespoons freshly squeezed lemon juice
½ teaspoon orange zest
½ teaspoon lime zest
½ teaspoon lemon zest
1 tablespoon maple syrup
¼ cup avocado or grapeseed oil
4 cups torn romaine
1 large avocado, cubed
1 cup flaked smoked salmon (about 6 ounces)

HERB SALAD AND ANCHOVY-SHALLOT VINAIGRETTE

I love herbs—they are the one ingredient that can turn any meal into a wow. For this salad, we flip the proportions and use mostly green leafy herbs, tossing in a few mixed greens for body. You can mix and match the herbs and quantities, using more of one and less of another, but this is my favorite mix that is balanced and exciting. I kept the vinaigrette simple but flavorful, allowing the herbaceous flavors to shine through—the anchovies work in harmony with the herbs.

▶ In a large bowl, combine the greens, parsley, cilantro, mint, tarragon, fennel, dill, and basil and toss so they are well blended. In a blender on high speed, blend the anchovy, vinegar, shallot, and mustard. While the blender is running, shake the blender so the ingredients fall to the center if need be. Pour in the oil in a slow stream to emulsify. When the vinaigrette is thick and comes together, stop the machine and scrap half of the vinaigrette onto the greens. Toss well until combined. Add salt, pepper, and more vinaigrette to taste and serve.

MAKES 4 TO 6 SERVINGS

2 cups mixed spring greens
1 cup fresh parsley leaves
½ cup fresh cilantro leaves
½ cup fresh mint leaves
¼ cup fresh tarragon or chervil leaves
¼ cup fennel fronds
¼ cup fresh dill, roughly chopped
¼ cup fresh basil
3 anchovy fillets
3 tablespoons red wine vinegar
1 tablespoon minced shallot
1 teaspoon Dijon mustard
½ cup extra-virgin olive oil
Kosher salt and freshly ground black pepper

CHAPTER EIGHT

salads for a crowd

COOKING FOR A CROWD IS A juggling act of timing everything. If you're having people over, you want a menu that can be made mostly ahead so that you are not stuck in the kitchen while guests are gathering. Other times cooking for a crowd demands you make a salad in advance and take it somewhere—think potlucks, picnics, and dinner parties. For all variables in feeding the masses, these salads were designed with holdover in mind—you can make them two to three hours ahead (and often prep the day before) without fear of the salad wilting into a soggy heap.

Certain vegetables are better than others when cooking for crowds. Those with strong structures do well—stalks, stems, and hearty greens. It's the web of cellulose in plants that keep them firm. Most vegetables from the cruciferous family are wonderful choices. Cabbage, broccoli, brussels sprouts, kale—all of these have strong, structured leaves that can sit in acid for some time before going limp. Fruit of plants, too, make for sturdy choices. Green beans, eggplants, and corn can all withstand long soaks in a bath of vinaigrette without adversely affecting their texture and flavor.

Keeping vegetables raw ensures they maintain a crisp bite, but sometimes roasting in advance produces a luscious, velvety quality. In particular, eggplant is a wonderful veg to roast and toss in vinaigrette. As it sits in the dressing, the flavors are absorbed into the flesh and this summer veg turns silky.

Whether raw or cooked, these salads are long-standing winners. Cut any recipe in half for a smaller group of people, or double it if you're serving the masses. And, as always, institute the cardinal rule—taste as you go and adjust the seasonings and vinaigrette proportions to your liking.

SNAP PEA AND POTATO
with Mustard Vinaigrette

This salad is as affordable as it is delicious. Perfect in early spring, when there is not much by way of local greens, baby potatoes are tossed with whole snap peas, pods and all, and doused in a bracing and punchy vinaigrette. Use whatever tender herbs you can get your hands on—chervil, tarragon, cilantro, and chives all work well. Here, warm potatoes soak up the vinaigrette and help break down chewy pea pods—a perfect marriage of spring vegetables.

MAKES 4 TO 6 SERVINGS

½ pound small waxy potatoes (round yellow, Yukon Gold, or Red Bliss)
2 tablespoons kosher salt, plus more for seasoning
2 tablespoons minced shallot
2 tablespoons red wine vinegar
6 tablespoons extra-virgin olive oil
1 tablespoon Dijon mustard
¼ teaspoon freshly ground black pepper, plus more for seasoning
½ pound sugar snap peas (about 2 cups), chopped
½ cup chopped fresh parsley
½ cup chopped fresh dill
4 cups arugula or other sturdy greens (kales, mustards, etc.)

▶ Peel the potatoes and submerge them immediately in a large bowl of cool water. Once all the potatoes are peeled, move them to a large pot and cover them with cold water. Add the salt and bring the potatoes to a boil over high heat. Reduce the heat slightly, and cook until the potatoes are just tender, 5 to 20 minutes.

▶ While the potatoes are cooking, in a large salad bowl, put the shallots and vinegar and let it sit for 5 minutes to macerate. Add the oil, mustard, and pepper and stir well with a fork to emulsify the oil with the vinegar and mustard.

▶ Once the potatoes are tender, drain them, reserving ¼ cup of the cooking liquid. Break the potatoes in half, using your hands, so there are rough edges that soak up the vinaigrette. While the potatoes are still warm, add them and the reserved cooking liquid to the salad bowl and, using a large spoon, fold gently to combine. Season to taste with salt and pepper and add the snap peas, parsley, dill, and greens and fold gently once. Leave covered on the countertop until ready to serve.

RAW ASPARAGUS
with Pecorino and Pine Nuts

This is one of my favorite salads. It is simple, delicious, and elegant—a beautiful salad to prepare for a special meal. We don't often see asparagus served raw, but the tender stalks are actually pretty tasty and crispy when eaten raw. The nutty flavor is pronounced, and they hold their crisp quality, making them perfect for crowds and make-ahead bowls of salad. Opt for thicker spears, making it easier to shave off ribbons of salad.

MAKES 8 SERVINGS

2 pounds large asparagus
¼ cup extra-virgin olive oil
3 tablespoons freshly
   squeezed lemon juice
Kosher salt and freshly
   ground black pepper
6 ounces shaved pecorino
1 cup toasted pine nuts

▶ Hold the asparagus up by the tip in one hand, and using a vegetable peeler, shave off long, thin strips. As the tips are tender, go slowly or snap them off and add them to the bowl whole. When all the asparagus are shaved, add the oil and lemon juice and fold gently to coat. Season to taste with salt and pepper.

▶ On a large platter, place the salad, scatter the pecorino and pine nuts over the top, and serve.

SHAVED BRUSSELS SPROUTS, CANDIED WALNUTS, AND PECORINO

Shaved brussels sprouts make for a hearty and surprising salad—most people expect brussels sprouts to be cooked. Shaved thinly, brussels sprouts are tender and won't break down quickly in acids, making them an ideal choice for crowds and make-ahead salads. For quick prep, use the slicing disc on your food processor—shredding all these sprouts will take seconds. If you don't have a food processor, get ready for some chopping! Take your time and make the slices as thin as possible.

▶ To make the vinaigrette, in a medium bowl, put the lemon juice, mustard, and shallot and let the shallots macerate, about 20 minutes. Whisk in the olive oil and maple syrup until well combined and emulsified. Season to taste with salt and pepper and set aside.

▶ To make the candied walnuts, cover the bottom of a large, deep-sided sauté pan with the peanut oil; let it pool a bit. Heat the pan over medium-high heat, and when the oil begins to ripple slightly, add the walnuts, stirring continuously so they don't burn. When the walnuts start to smoke and brown, add ½ cup of the sugar and toss, toss, toss! You don't want to burn that sugar.

▶ After the sugar is dissolved and the nuts are well coated, 3 to 4 minutes, use a slotted spoon to put the nuts in a glass bowl with the remaining ¼ cup sugar and a good pinch of salt. Working quickly, stir to combine and then set aside to cool. Once the nuts are cool, remove them from the bowl, leaving behind any residual sugar.

▶ To compose the salad, add the brussels sprouts and pecorino to the vinaigrette and fold to combine well. Season to taste with salt and pepper. On a large platter, place the salad, sprinkle with the candied walnuts, and serve.

MAKES 6 TO 8 SERVINGS

FOR THE VINAIGRETTE:
¼ cup freshly squeezed lemon juice (from 2 medium lemons)
2 tablespoons Dijon mustard
2 tablespoons minced shallot
½ cup extra-virgin olive oil
1 tablespoon maple syrup
Kosher salt and freshly ground black pepper

½ cup peanut oil
2 cups walnuts
¾ cup sugar, divided
Kosher salt
1½ pounds brussels sprouts, shredded
1 cup finely grated pecorino
Freshly ground black pepper

NAPA CABBAGE AND APPLES
with Basil-Lime Vinaigrette

This salad is refreshing and versatile. Less chewy than green cabbage, Napa cabbage is soft and frilly. This light salad can be served on its own as a side salad, or act as a filler for sandwiches and tacos alike. I make a half batch and use it as a garnish over stews and soup, or add some avocado and leftover roast chicken for a more robust and quick weekday meal. Be sure to use a mandoline if you have one, or a sharp knife, and take your time, getting the cabbage as thin as possible.

► In a large jar or blender, put the oil, vinegar, honey, lime juice and zest, mustard, cayenne, and salt. Shake vigorously or blend on high speed until well blended and emulsified. Add the vinaigrette to a large salad bowl and stir in the basil.

► To the bowl, add the cabbage and apples and toss the ingredients, using both hands or a large spoon. I like to use my hands, ensuring the whole salad gets dressed. Stir very well until the ingredients are well combined and the cabbage is evenly coated. Set aside for at least 30 minutes. Season to taste with salt and pepper and serve.

MAKES 6 TO 8 SERVINGS

½ cup extra-virgin olive oil
3 tablespoons apple cider vinegar
2 tablespoons honey
2 tablespoons freshly squeezed lime juice
Zest from ½ medium lime
2 teaspoons Dijon mustard
½ teaspoon ground cayenne pepper
1 teaspoon kosher salt, plus more for seasoning
¼ cup chopped fresh basil
1 medium head Napa cabbage (about 1½ to 2 pounds), cored and shredded
6 medium apples (Pink Lady, Empire, Honeycrisp, etc.), cored and thinly julienned
Freshly ground black pepper

SWEET CORN
with Cherry Tomatoes, Avocado, and Basil

This is one of my all-time favorite summer salads, and it is so unbelievably simple that I am betting it becomes a favorite of yours too. It's great served with anything from the grill or as a fresh, light side dish. In-season corn is paired with ripe tomatoes and creamy avocados for a harmonious blend and colorful dish. For a different variation and some heat, add chopped jalapeño. Or swap out the basil for a mix of herbs. Or add some grilled green onions! This is a fabulous salad to add to your summer lineup.

MAKES 6 TO 8 SERVINGS

6 ears sweet corn, husked
2 pints cherry tomatoes, halved
2 medium avocados, cut into 1-inch cubes
½ cup chopped fresh basil
½ cup extra-virgin olive oil
¼ cup apple cider vinegar
Kosher salt and freshly ground black pepper

▶ Fill a large pot with a lid with 1 inch of water and bring it to a boil over high heat. While the water is coming to a boil, prepare an ice water bath—add several ice cubes to a large bowl of cold water and set aside. When the water is boiling, add the ears of corn (breaking them in half if you need to make them fit), cover, and reduce the heat to medium. Steam for 6 minutes. Remove the pot from the heat, and using tongs, put the corn directly into the ice water bath until cool, 3 to 4 minutes.

▶ When the corn is cool enough to handle, use a sharp knife to cut the kernels from the corn cob by scraping them with the knife lengthwise. (Set the flat base of the cob against the cutting board for stability.)

▶ In a large salad bowl, put the corn kernels, tomatoes, avocado, and basil. Add the oil and vinegar and stir until well coated. Season to taste with salt and pepper.

ROASTED EGGPLANT
with Cilantro Vinaigrette

A perfect accompaniment to grilled foods, this rich-tasting eggplant comes bathed in a pungent vinaigrette spiked with fish sauce. Tossed in olive oil and roasted, eggplant turns supple and has a concentrated flavor that I love. Filling and satiating, this summer fruit makes for a side dish that holds its flavor for hours, even in the sun and heat. I often make a half batch just for myself and eat it for a quick meal over a day or two. The flavors develop as the eggplant marinates, so it's a perfect choice for long meals, make-ahead recipes, or a backyard barbecue with friends. The vinaigrette is meant to be plentiful, and this salad is strongly flavored, so save any extra for another salad or cut it with some olive oil and dress a bowl of greens.

▶ Preheat the oven to 375 degrees F.
▶ In a large mixing bowl, put the eggplant and drizzle with the oil, mixing well to coat each piece. Put the eggplant on a parchment-lined baking sheet, cut side down, and roast in the oven for 20 to 30 minutes, or until the eggplant is deep brown on one side.
▶ While the eggplant is roasting, make the vinaigrette. In a large mixing bowl, combine the onion, fish sauce, lime juice, shallot, cilantro, sugar, and chili flakes. Use a whisk to dissolve the sugar.
▶ When the eggplant is nicely brown, remove it from the oven and add it immediately to the vinaigrette. Using a spatula, gently fold the eggplant into the vinaigrette so all the pieces are evenly coated. Set aside for 10 minutes. This allows the flavors to infuse and develop. Garnish with the pomegranate seeds and serve.

MAKES 6 TO 8 SERVINGS

3 pounds small Asian eggplant, stemmed and halved lengthwise, then cut into 4-inch-long pieces
2 tablespoons extra-virgin olive oil

FOR THE CILANTRO VINAIGRETTE:
4 green onions, thinly sliced
6 tablespoons fish sauce
6 tablespoons freshly squeezed lime juice (from about 2 limes)
¼ cup minced shallot
¼ cup chopped fresh cilantro
2 tablespoons sugar
4 teaspoons red chili flakes

1 cup pomegranate seeds (from about ½ pomegranate) (optional)

CORIANDER FLANK STEAK AND RHUBARB VINAIGRETTE

Rhubarb stalks make for excellent purees, adding texture and flavor to thick dressings. Here, cooked and pureed rhubarb is seasoned and then paired with hearty arugula and rich pieces of steak in a tossed salad. The addition of toasted croutons and blue cheese makes this fit for a meal.

MAKES 6 SERVINGS

2 stalks rhubarb, chopped (about 2 cups)
1 tablespoon maple syrup
1 teaspoon Dijon mustard
6 tablespoons avocado or grapeseed oil, divided
1 pound flank steak
Kosher salt and freshly ground black pepper
2 teaspoons ground coriander
6 cups arugula or salad greens
2 cups "croutons" (day-old bread cut into 1-inch cubes and grilled or broiled until toasted)
6 ounces blue cheese, crumbled
Parsley leaves (optional)
Celery leaves (optional)

▶ To make the vinaigrette, in a small saucepan, add ½ cup water and the rhubarb, cover, and bring to a boil over high heat. Once the water is boiling, reduce the heat to a simmer and cook until the rhubarb is soft and falling apart, about 15 minutes. Drain the rhubarb from the water, and in a blender on high speed, combine the rhubarb mash, maple syrup, and mustard. Slowly pour in 4 tablespoons of the oil until the vinaigrette has emulsified, about 30 seconds. Set aside.

▶ Place the oven rack at the top position—about 6 inches from the broiler coils—and heat the broiler. Season the steak on both sides with the salt, pepper, and coriander and coat with the remaining 2 tablespoons oil. Lay the steak flat on a baking sheet, place it in the oven, and bake until the steak is brown, about 6 minutes.

▶ Flip the steak over and cook the other side under the broiler until just charred and cooked to medium rare, 6 minutes more. Remove the steak from the oven and let rest it for 10 minutes before slicing it into ½-inch-thick pieces, cutting across the grain.

▶ In a large bowl, add the arugula, croutons, cheese, and half of the vinaigrette. Add the parsley and celery leaves, and toss to combine well. Season to taste with salt and pepper, and divide evenly, adding several slices of steak over each before serving.

SHAVED CABBAGE AND WHITE ONION
with Pomegranate and Orange-Caraway Dressing

Cabbage is a cruciferous vegetable that is high in sulfur and therefore encourages your body to produce antioxidant and detoxification proteins. It's a wonder veg! Winter slaws offer a perfect way to freshen up the typically heavy dishes that predominate when the weather turns cold. In this slaw thinly shaved cabbage is paired with sweet onion and pomegranate seeds for a juicy pop and some color. Slaws are best left to macerate for some time before serving, so plan ahead and let this one rest at least a few hours before the meal. You can play with the flavor profile by adding chopped cilantro, a pinch of cayenne pepper, or a handful of raisins, and this salad can, of course, be made in summer months for outdoor eating or picnic meals—cabbage holds its crunch even in the heat.

MAKES 6 TO 8 SERVINGS

- 1 pound white cabbage, cored
- ½ medium white onion, peeled
- ½ cup extra-virgin olive oil
- ¼ cup freshly squeezed orange juice (from 1 large orange)
- 2 tablespoons rice wine vinegar
- 2 tablespoons caraway seeds, crushed in a mortar and pestle
- 1 cup pomegranate seeds (from about ½ pomegranate)
- 1 cup crumbled feta
- ½ cup whole fresh mint leaves

▶ Using a sharp knife and working slowly, cut the cabbage into very thin slices—almost shaving them off. The thinner you slice the cabbage, the more appetizing it is. Cut the onion in the same fashion, getting it as thin as possible. Set both aside.

▶ In a large bowl, put the oil, orange juice, vinegar, and caraway seeds and stir well to combine. Add the cabbage and onions and toss well to combine. Cover the bowl with a plate or plastic wrap and set aside on the counter or in the refrigerator for at least 1 hour. Just before serving, stir in the pomegranate seeds. Pour the salad onto a platter or move to a shallow bowl, sprinkle the feta and mint evenly over the top, and serve.

GREEN BEANS, TOASTED HAZELNUTS, AND YOGURT-DILL DRESSING

Green beans hold their firmness and shape for days, so they are the perfect choice for serving crowds, allowing home cooks to work many steps ahead of time and have the salad waiting. Choose thin green beans for this salad—they are tenderer and often sweeter than older, more fibrous beans. While a creamy dressing is used here, this salad can be easily updated with a mustard vinaigrette or a miso-based dressing (see page 180)—feel free to update it and make it your own.

MAKES 6 TO 8 SERVINGS

Kosher salt
2 pounds fresh green beans
(haricots verts, romanos,
green wax beans, etc.)

FOR THE YOGURT-DILL
DRESSING:
½ cup plain yogurt
¼ cup extra-virgin olive oil
¼ cup chopped fresh dill
Kosher salt and freshly
ground black pepper

1 cup toasted and finely
chopped hazelnuts

▶ To prepare the green beans, bring a large pot of water to a boil over high heat and season with salt. While the water is coming to a boil, prepare an ice water bath—add several ice cubes to a large bowl of cold water and set aside. Add the green beans to the boiling water, working in batches, and blanch for 2 to 4 minutes, stirring occasionally. Using a slotted spoon, remove the beans from the pot and plunge them into the ice water bath, allowing them to cool 1 to 2 minutes.

▶ Strain the green beans from the water and pat dry.

▶ To make the dressing, in a large bowl, put the yogurt, oil, and dill and stir vigorously until well combined. Season to taste with salt and pepper, then add the green beans and fold until all are well coated. Season to taste again with salt and pepper. Move the beans to a large platter, sprinkle with the hazelnuts, and serve.

cooling salads

COOLING FLAVORS EMBODY EVERYTHING we think about when we crave salads—a plate of something refreshing and cool, a bite to relieve heat, a light meal. By nature lettuce is cooling, particularly wide-ribbed, white-leafed varieties like romaine and iceberg that pack water into their big cells and are hydrating. Other members of the cooling food family are cucumbers, mint, celery, spinach, and zucchini. Fully ripe fruits—melons, grapes, mangoes—are often cooling as well. Avoid the foods that cause heat within the body, such as ginger, hot peppers, and mustard greens.

Cucumbers and melons are members of the same plant family, and all have fruits that contain a high water content, making them a refreshing choice. These fruits add crispness to recipes and are healthy powerhouses helping regulate blood pressure and maintain a body's hydration.

In addition to vegetables, dairy-based ingredients are thought to be cooling. The Indian condiment *raita* (a mix of yogurt and cucumber) is used specifically to cool down spice from their culturally aromatic food. Mango *lassi*, a mango-yogurt beverage, is also cooling and popular in India, where temperatures soar.

Pair cooling salads with simple foods like grilled fish. Of course, these salads can also complement heavy meals, offsetting the richness. The cucumber-onion-dill combination is a perfect accompaniment at a summer barbecue, next to a plate of grilled steak or ribs.

You can also use the cooling salads as garnish for other recipes. Try dolloping a spoonful of cooling salad on soup as a refreshing topper. The fennel shavings in the salted fennel salad (see page 164) are lovely over a bowl of hot bean soup. On really hot days, I'll reach for the melon and cucumber with prawns salad (see page 167) that is full of healthy fat and protein but light enough that it will not slow me down.

LITTLE GEM LETTUCE
with Shrimp and Coconut-Avocado Dressing

This salad is nutritional perfection, and I lean on it often when I'm short on time and looking for a clean-eating option. Simply steamed shrimp and crispy Little Gem lettuce is doused in a luxurious and creamy dressing made from avocado and coconut milk—a winning combination of good fats. (Be sure to choose coconut milk, not coconut cream.) Little Gem lettuce is a cute name for what is essentially really small heads of romaine. Their leaves tend to be deeply wrinkled and the hearts are crispy and strong—a nice counterpoint to the rich dressing.

MAKES 4 SERVINGS

1 pound shrimp, shelled and thawed
1 pound Little Gem lettuce (about 4 heads), cut into 1-inch-thick ribbons
1 large ripe avocado
¼ cup coconut milk
2 tablespoons grapeseed or avocado oil
2 tablespoons freshly squeezed lime juice
Kosher salt and freshly ground black pepper

▶ To cook the shrimp, in a medium pot with a lid over high heat, heat 1 inch of water. While the water is coming to a boil, prepare an ice water bath—add several ice cubes to a large bowl of cold water and set aside. Once the water is boiling, add the shrimp and cook until they are pink in color and cooked through, 2 to 3 minutes. Remove the shrimp from the heat and drain, plunging them into the ice water bath to halt any further cooking. Once the shrimp are cool, drain them from the cold water and set aside until ready to use.

▶ In a large bowl, put the lettuce and set aside.

▶ In a blender on high speed, blend the avocado, coconut milk, oil, and lime juice until well blended and smooth. If the blender stalls because the mixture is too thick, add a small bit of water—2 tablespoons to start and more only as needed to thoroughly blend.

▶ Using a rubber spatula, scrape all the dressing into a small bowl. Season to taste with salt and pepper before spooning half the mixture over the lettuce. Toss the salad to coat, adding more dressing as necessary. Finally, add the shrimp, toss to combine, and serve.

SALTED FENNEL, MEYER LEMON, MINT, AND SHALLOT

Shaved fennel bulb is one of the most refreshing ingredients there is. Soaking it in lightly salted water first ups the crispiness and adds to the lightness of this salad. If you don't have a mandoline to shave the fennel, use a sharp knife and work slowly to get the thinnest cut possible. Meyer lemons are sweeter than the more traditional Eureka lemons, and their flavor is subtle. Though Meyer lemons are still pungent, your lips will not pucker while eating them! This is an enlivening winter salad to perk you up during dark days.

► Fill a large bowl halfway with water and add two handfuls of ice cubes. Sprinkle in salt until the water is lightly salted and add the fennel shavings, letting them sit in the water for 10 to 20 minutes. Strain the fennel and pat it dry with a paper towel.
► In a large bowl, put the fennel, lemon slices, mint, oil, and vinegar. Stir gently until combined well. Season to taste with salt and pepper and serve.

MAKES 4 SERVINGS

Kosher salt
1 small or ½ large fennel bulb, cored and shaved (about 2½ cups)
1 large Meyer lemon, or 2 small lemons, rinds removed, seeded, and cut crosswise into rounds
½ cup whole fresh mint leaves
3 tablespoons extra-virgin olive oil
1 tablespoon rice wine vinegar
Freshly ground black pepper

MELON AND CUCUMBER
with Prawns and Avocado Cream

Melon and cucumber are like peas and carrots, and both are nutritional powerhouses in ways that leafy greens are not. Both are packed with potassium, and honeydew is an anticoagulant (so good for heart health) while cucumbers are one of the best diuretics you can eat. What's not to love? Paired with healthy-fat avocado and the lean protein of prawns, this salad makes a wonderful summertime lunch.

▶ To cook the prawns, in a medium pot with a lid over high heat, heat 1 inch of water. While the water is coming to a boil, prepare an ice water bath—add several ice cubes to a large bowl of cold water and set aside. Once the water is boiling, add the prawns and cook until they are pink in color and cooked through, 2 to 3 minutes. Remove the prawns from the heat and drain, plunging them into the ice water bath to halt any further cooking. Once the prawns are cool, drain them from the cold water and set aside until ready to use.

▶ In a large bowl, put the cucumber, melon, and mint and set aside.

▶ In a blender on high speed, blend the avocado, yogurt, oil, lime juice, and honey until well blended and smooth. If the blender stalls because the mixture is too thick, add a small bit of water—2 tablespoons to start and more only as needed to thoroughly blend.

▶ Using a rubber spatula, scrape all the dressing into a small bowl. Season to taste with salt and pepper before spooning half the mixture over the salad. Toss the salad to coat, adding more dressing as necessary. Finally, add the prawns, toss to combine, and serve.

MAKES 4 SERVINGS

1 pound frozen prawns, shelled and thawed
1 English cucumber, cubed (about 2 cups)
½ medium honeydew melon, cubed (about 2 cups)
1 tablespoon chopped fresh mint leaves
1 medium avocado
¼ cup plain yogurt
2 tablespoons grapeseed or avocado oil
2 tablespoons freshly squeezed lime juice
1 tablespoon honey
Kosher salt and freshly ground black pepper

CUCUMBER AND ONION
with Yogurt-Dill Dressing

Hitting all the cool notes, this salad is flavorful, cooling, and budget friendly. In this eastern European salad, cucumbers and onions are sliced super thin and lightly pickled in vinegar overnight. From there they are strained and tossed with cooling yogurt-dill dressing that is creamy and satisfying. It makes an excellent side salad on its own or works beautifully next to grilled meats and fish.

▶ In a large sealable container (or a resealable plastic bag), put the cucumbers and onions. Pour in the vinegar, oil, and honey and cover. Shake vigorously until all the cucumbers and onions are well coated and put it in the refrigerator overnight or for at least 6 hours.

▶ Before serving, strain any brine from the bag, reserving 2 tablespoons. In a large bowl, put the mixture and add the yogurt, dill, and reserved brine and fold to combine until well blended and no yogurt lumps are left. Season to taste with salt and pepper and serve.

MAKES 6 TO 8 SERVINGS

4 cucumbers, peeled and sliced paper thin
1 small white onion, cut super thin into half moons
¼ cup distilled white vinegar
2 tablespoons extra-virgin olive oil
¼ teaspoon honey
¼ cup plain yogurt
2 tablespoons fresh dill
Kosher salt and freshly ground black pepper

HOMEGROWN SPROUTS

SPROUTS ARE GERMINATED EDIBLE SEEDS. Seeds store all the energy and food they need to produce healthy plants. By eating them at a very early stage of growth, we reap the rewards of all that good energy. Sprouted seeds are phenomenally nutritious. The process of sprouting increases the vitamin content of seeds significantly. All sprouts contain more vitamin C than an orange, pound for pound, and are a source of a long list of nutrients and vitamins. Many legume sprouts contain a complete protein, making them an excellent choice for vegetarians.

Sprouts add a fresh, crispy texture to salads and are easy to grow at home. You can add a handful of sprouts to any of these recipes with good results. They are particularly delicious with grain bowls, as they add nutrition and texture, and in winter salads they supply high-impact nutrients during a season in which our green leafy options are limited.

Different sprouts will carry different flavors, of course. Legumes like peas or mung beans grow into thick, crunchy sprouts that do not produce green leaves. Broccoli and alfalfa sprouts are more delicate and have an earthy flavor, and are among those that contain chlorophyll and develop green leaves. When selecting what to sprout, make sure to purchase organic seed.

You need only a quart-size glass to get going, which will hold about 2 tablespoons of seed successfully. Light is not necessary to sprout seeds, but you do need to keep them warm and moist. Filtered water is preferred.

TO GROW SPROUTS:

▶ Soak the seeds for a few hours in a few inches of water—larger seeds may need to be soaked overnight. After soaking, drain out the water, rinse the seeds in fresh water, and drain them again. Make sure you don't leave a pool of water in the jar. (You can leave the jar upside down, covered in a piece of cheesecloth, to ensure drainage.)

Once drained completely but still moist, cover the jar with a thick layer of cheesecloth, secure with a rubber band, and turn the jar on its side to allow for sprouting room and air circulation.

▶ Rinse the jar with fresh water two or three times a day, every day. Drain well each time and set it back on its side. The sprouts should be ready to harvest in 3 to 5 days. Taste them after every rinse to see when the flavor has developed to your taste. When done, fill the jar with water for the last time and remove any thick hulls (the outer covering of the seeds) that float to the top. Drain the sprouts in a colander and eat immediately, or wrap in a single layer of dish towel or paper towel and hold in the refrigerator, where they will keep for 3 to 4 days.

JICAMA AND AVOCADO
with Cilantro Vinaigrette

I made a version of this salad from Rick Bayless several years ago for a Fourth of July party and everyone raved. We tend to overlook jicama in the United States—it is an uncommon root vegetable that is native to Mexico, but it has a sweet-starchy quality that is refreshing and filling, and this tuber is packed with potassium and vitamin C. A thin vinaigrette is made from blending cilantro with lime juice and chilies, and it's excellent on many salads, so I always make a double batch and save some for another day. Anaheim chilies tend to have less heat than most, but use jalapeño or serrano if you'd like to turn up the heat.

▶ To make the vinaigrette, in a blender on high speed, blend the cilantro, chili, lime juice and zest, and honey until well combined. With the blender still running on high, drizzle in the oil until the vinaigrette is emulsified, about 30 seconds. Set aside.

▶ In a large bowl, put the jicama, spinach, romaine, and avocado. Pour in half the vinaigrette and toss to combine. Add more vinaigrette as needed. Season to taste with salt and pepper and serve.

MAKES 4 SERVINGS

FOR THE CILANTRO VINAIGRETTE:
½ cup fresh cilantro leaves and stems
1 small Anaheim chili, seeded and chopped
⅓ cup freshly squeezed lime juice (from 2 large limes)
1 teaspoon lime zest
1 teaspoon honey
¾ cup extra-virgin olive oil

1 medium jicama, peeled and cut into matchsticks
2 cups spinach leaves
1 cup romaine or mixed greens
1 large avocado, cubed
Kosher salt and freshly ground black pepper

BUTTER LETTUCE
with Fresh Coconut, Mango, and Cashew Dressing

This salad has many cooling flavors, making it an excellent choice for a hot day or to cool fiery digestion in cooler months. Young coconut is available in gourmet grocery stores, like Whole Foods, and Asian markets where it is often less expensive. Use a large spoon to scoop the jellylike and fleshy meat out of young coconuts—it's easy to do and will be intuitive.

▶ To make the vinaigrette, in a small bowl, add the cashews, honey, cumin, and ½ cup of the reserved coconut water and let sit for 20 to 30 minutes. In a blender on high speed, puree the cashew mixture until smooth and creamy. Season to taste with salt and pepper and set aside until ready to use.

▶ In a large bowl, put the lettuce, spinach, mango, coconut meat, and half of the dressing. Fold to combine and season to taste with salt and pepper. Add more dressing, if desired, and serve.

MAKES 4 SERVINGS

½ cup raw cashews
1 teaspoon honey
¼ teaspoon ground cumin
1 young coconut, meat scooped out and cut into strips and water reserved
Kosher salt and freshly ground black pepper
1 medium head butter lettuce, leaves torn into large strips
2 cups spinach leaves
1 large mango, peeled and diced

ZUCCHINI NOODLES
with Feta and Lemon

Everyone has been raving about the spiralizer for years now, and I finally broke down and bought one after so many good meals. A spiralizer is a hand-cranked kitchen gadget that turns fruits and vegetables into noodle shapes, ribbons, and more. I love the noodle fitting and use it often to produce pasta-like strands of raw vegetables for salads. Here, zucchini gets cranked into long noodles and tossed with a refreshing mix of mint and basil—perfect summertime fare. Of course, if you're not up for running out to purchase a new kitchen toy, you can always make zucchini ribbons by using a mandoline or vegetable peeler.

MAKES 4 SERVINGS

¼ cup pine nuts
3 tablespoons extra-virgin olive oil
1 tablespoon freshly squeezed lemon juice
1 teaspoon lemon zest
1 pound zucchini (2 to 3 medium zucchinis)
2 tablespoons chopped fresh basil
1 tablespoon chopped fresh mint leaves
½ teaspoon kosher salt
3 ounces feta, crumbled

▶ In a medium sauté pan over medium-high heat, toast the pine nuts, stirring continuously until they are golden on all sides and you can smell them toasting, 3 to 5 minutes. Remove the pan from the heat and put the pine nuts on a small plate to cool. Set aside until ready to use.

▶ In a medium bowl, stir together the oil and lemon juice and zest. Set aside. Trim the ends of the zucchinis to remove any discolored portions, leaving the stem intact. Using the spiralizer, make long noodles, cutting them every 4 inches or so and letting them fall into the bowl with oil and lemon. Fold to coat the zucchini noodles. Work quickly, as this dressing helps keep the zucchini from turning brown prior to serving.

▶ Add the basil, mint, salt, and pine nuts to the salad bowl. Fold once or twice until just combined. Transfer the salad to a serving platter or a large, shallow bowl and sprinkle the feta on top. Serve immediately.

LITTLE GEM AND CILANTRO SALAD
with Watermelon Vinaigrette

Little Gem lettuce is like baby romaine. It is firm in texture but has a smaller rib, which I prefer, and is deeply creviced and crinkly, adding crunch to a salad. This recipe makes a large portion of dressing, as watermelon varies in its juiciness. Leftovers will store well in the refrigerator for several days, so hold any residual for another salad. I love this salad for its delicate flavors—cool cilantro and creamy avocado.

MAKES 4 SERVINGS

2 cups cubed watermelon, seeded
¼ cup rice wine vinegar
1 teaspoon honey
½ cup extra-virgin olive oil
Kosher salt and freshly ground black pepper (optional)
2 heads Little Gem lettuce, leaves removed from core and left whole
½ cup cilantro leaves
1 large ripe avocado, cubed

▶ In a blender on high speed, puree the watermelon until smooth. (You may need to add a tablespoon of water to get the fruit going.) Add the vinegar and honey and puree again until the pulp is a thin, pourable puree, about 1 minute. Pour the watermelon mixture into a fine-mesh sieve, filtering out any seeds and chunks of watermelon. With the blender running, drizzle in the oil until well blended and emulsified. Season to taste with salt and pepper.

▶ In a large bowl, put the lettuce, cilantro, and avocado and pour in half the vinaigrette. Fold gently to coat, adding more vinaigrette as needed. Season to taste with salt and pepper and serve.

vinaigrettes & dressings

VINAIGRETTE OR DRESSING IS ARGUABLY the most important part of a salad. A killer dressing will make any green taste great. A perfectly dressed salad can go from satisfactory to sublime. Although a simple drizzle of olive oil with a squeeze of fresh lemon juice and a pinch of salt and pepper should definitely not be overlooked, options for vinaigrettes are truly infinite.

Vinaigrette has a typical proportion of one part acid to three parts oil. In essence, one tablespoon lemon juice blended with three tablespoons of olive oil allows for a harmonious mix of acid and fat. This is a great equation to bear in mind when improvising.

The real fun comes, however, when you start playing with acids and fats. All vinegars and citrus juices are acidic. The flavor of acid in a dressing can be altered simply by changing the citrus from lemon to orange or lime. You can also try a number of vinegars or use pickling juice from your preserves. Acids also come in the form of juices. If you have a vegetable juicer at home, fresh-pressed and tangy rhubarb juice makes pungent vinaigrette. Apple juice from pressed green apples (young apples) can also be substituted, as can fresh-pressed tomato juice or juice squeezed from tomatillos.

Oils, too, offer a variety of flavorful choices. Many salads you eat at restaurants and cafés are made with a neutral oil such as grapeseed oil. This oil does not have a strong flavor and maintains a nice emulsion. It is also affordable. Olive oil, too, is very popular and can either be neutral tasting or flavored strongly of black pepper and grass.

The fat in a salad dressing can be replaced with other rich ingredients—nut oils (sesame or walnut), eggs (raw or hard-boiled and mashed), or avocado. Same goes for oils pressed from seeds—pumpkin seed oil is gaining in popularity and is an easy-to-find choice.

Flavors can be added from spices, alliums, herbs, and more. A few drops of fish sauce contributes umami—considered the fifth taste. And while traditional vinaigrette is made with Dijon mustard, you can add flavors simply by including a handful of chopped herbs, some fresh grated ginger, or chopped shallots. A little sweetness in vinaigrette mellows out the acidity and softens the flavor. Try adding a teaspoon of honey, some fruit syrup from your canned preserves, maple syrup, or molasses.

HOMEMADE HERB VINEGAR

IF YOU HAVE LEFTOVER HERBS OR A PROLIFIC plant that needs cutting back, you can dry herbs for your spice cupboard or use them to flavor vinegar. Herb vinegars are made of two simple ingredients—vinegar and fresh herbs—and can be made in minutes. Subtle in flavor, herb vinegars impart an undertone of herb along with the tang of vinegar. They can be used in salads and vinaigrettes.

Use fresh, healthy sprigs and any clear vinegar for the best results—I love both champagne and rice wine vinegar. Any herb can work—try mint, lemon balm, basil, or tarragon. Wash and dry jars of any size, just so long as they have a cap or lid and the herb can be completely submerged. Glass containers that can be sealed with a lid or cork are perfect.

2 cups apple cider vinegar	4 to 6 stalks whole fresh herbs

▶ To make the infusion, in a medium sauce pan over high heat, heat the vinegar until it just begins to boil. Add the herbs directly to prepared jars (using two stalks of herb for every cup of vinegar if you're making larger quantities) and pour the hot vinegar over the herbs, leaving a bit of headspace. Cover the vinegar and store in a cool, dark place for 3 to 4 weeks, checking the flavor after 2 days. When the flavor is to your liking, strain and discard the herbs and store the infused vinegar in a cool, dark cupboard.

▶ Herb vinegars will keep for 3 months, longer if refrigerated. Be mindful of any mold or fermentation bubbles—this means the batch is spoiled and should be thrown out. As vinegar has a high acid content, there is no risk of botulism; mold and yeast are the two culprits of spoilage.

OIL AND VINEGAR

Basic vinaigrettes are hard to beat—they work with delicate greens, sturdy winter vegetables, grains, and even roast meats. Great foundational recipes to know and memorize, any of these vinaigrettes provide a jumping-off point for riffing. On their own, however, they are sheer perfection. All of the following recipes make enough vinaigrette to dress one medium-size salad that will serve four people—increase or decrease proportions as needed.

Red Wine Vinaigrette

A basic vinaigrette, this recipe is excellent on salads, for dressing grains, or even as a zingy drizzle over roasted meats. You can play with this by adding a handful of chopped herbs or alternating the vinegar. Try stone-ground mustard instead of Dijon for a slight variation.

3 tablespoons extra-virgin olive oil
1 tablespoon red wine vinegar
1 teaspoon Dijon mustard

Kosher salt and freshly ground
black pepper

▶ In a small jar, add the oil, vinegar, and mustard, cover, and shake to combine. Season to taste with salt and pepper. Store any extra vinaigrette in a covered glass jar in the refrigerator indefinitely.

Lemon Vinaigrette

You can sub out the citrus here, making this a good "recipe" to remember. This salad dressing is wonderful over a simple bowl of mixed greens—a great basic. Finish the bowl with a generous shaving of Parmesan, which adds salt, fat, and sharpness. For intense lemony flavor, skip the juice and zest, and mince half of a lemon (skin, membranes, and all) and mix with olive oil and crushed garlic.

2 tablespoons fresh lemon juice
1 tablespoon minced shallot
1 teaspoon lemon zest

3 tablespoons olive oil
Kosher salt and freshly ground
    black pepper

▶ In a small bowl, add the lemon juice, shallot, and lemon zest. Let sit for 10 minutes and then stir in the oil until well combined. You can also use a glass jar, or put everything over the top of salad greens and simply toss to combine. Season to taste with salt and pepper. Store any extra vinaigrette in a covered glass jar in the refrigerator for up to 3 days.

CREAMY DRESSINGS

Creamy dressings need not always be cream-based. Yogurt, nuts, and cheese make for smooth purees that are tasty and rich.

Yogurt Dressing

Yogurt is a wonderful salad dressing base, as it's tangy and rich. Using nonfat yogurt lowers the fat and calorie level of any salad too—a great cheat for anyone watching what they eat. Using a thick Greek-style yogurt turns this simple dressing into a dip for crudité. Alternate the flavor by adding spices or herbs, or try a tablespoon of pumpkin seed oil in place of the olive oil for nuttiness.

3 tablespoons yogurt
2 tablespoons extra-virgin olive
     or neutral oil

1 teaspoon honey
Kosher salt and freshly ground
     black pepper

▶ In a small jar, add the yogurt, oil, and honey, cover, and shake to combine. Season to taste with salt and pepper. Store any extra dressing in a covered glass jar in the refrigerator for up to 3 days.

Cashew-Cumin Dressing

Cashews puree into a thick cream, making an easy, healthy vegan recipe that can be used to dress salads. The nut meat breaks down into a smooth puree, whereas many other nuts produce a gritty texture when pureed. For a thicker dressing, add a few more nuts to the bowl, or a spoonful of cooked beans.

½ cup raw cashews
¼ cup boiling water
1 teaspoon honey

¼ teaspoon ground cumin
Kosher salt and freshly ground
     black pepper

▶ In a blender, puree the cashews, water, honey, and cumin until well combined and smooth. Season to taste with salt and pepper. Store any extra dressing in a covered glass jar in the refrigerator for up to 3 days.

Feta-Basil Dressing

Soft cheese can be loosened with yogurt or milk and turned into a silky, creamy dressing for salads or grain bowls. Here, salty feta is whipped with yogurt and spiked with basil to create a sultry summer dressing.

1½ cups crumbled feta
½ cup plain nonfat yogurt
2 tablespoons extra-virgin olive oil

Zest from 1 lemon
Milk, for thinning (optional)
¼ cup fresh basil

▶ In a food processor or strong blender, put the feta and yogurt and pulse to combine, 15 to 20 pulses. Add the oil and zest and blend to combine, about 1 minute. Thin with a few spoonfuls of milk. Add the basil and pulse until just mixed in and coarse, about 10 pulses. Remove the dressing from the food processor. Store any extra dressing in a covered glass jar in the refrigerator for up to 3 days.

FRUIT VINEGAR

PRESERVE THE SWEET FLAVOR OF SUMMER by preparing this simple fruit-infused vinegar. A fantastic addition to salads and meals, infused vinegar can also be added to a chilled glass of fizzy water as a drinking vinegar. You can make fruit vinegar simply by covering fresh fruit in vinegar and letting it macerate, moving the jar to a dark cupboard. This is a perfect method for days that you are short on time but must use the last of the fruit before it spoils.

When time allows, opt instead to cook the fruits quickly in hot vinegar, so they release all their juices into the jar. The extra effort produces a stellar product with a strong, identifiable taste. This fruit vinegar keeps well in the refrigerator for many months, thanks to the high acidity of both the fruit and the vinegar. This same process can be used for any summer fruit that releases juice readily—try strawberries, blackberries, peaches, or even mango!

MAKES ABOUT 1 CUP VINEGAR

1 quart fresh raspberries
1 cup red wine vinegar

½ cup sugar, plus more as needed

▶ In a medium shallow bowl, stir together the raspberries and vinegar. Cover with plastic wrap, setting the wrap directly on the surface of the mixture to help keep the berries submerged. Set aside on the countertop for 2 days.

▶ After 2 days, in a blender on high speed, puree the raspberry mixture until smooth. Set a fine-mesh sieve over a medium bowl. Using a rubber spatula, stir and push the raspberry mixture through the sieve, working to reserve the raspberry seeds. It takes about 5 minutes to get all the raspberry mixture through while leaving the seeds behind.

▶ In a medium saucepan over medium heat, put the berry puree and sugar. Bring to a low boil and cook, stirring often, until all the sugar has dissolved. Taste and add more sugar, if desired. Pour the raspberry-infused vinegar into a small glass bottle or jar and cool (uncovered at this point). Once the vinegar has cooled, cover and store in the refrigerator.

PUREED VEGETABLES

Many vegetables can be pureed in a food processor and turned into a velvety mash. This works with both cooked vegetables (see the zucchini hummus on page 58) or with raw vegetables or fruit that are high in starch and sugars.

Creamy Mustard-Carrot Vinaigrette

Raw carrots puree fairly easily into a creamy mash that clings to greens and salads. Here, fresh ginger and mustard add a tangy, hot note that cuts through hearty greens, grain bowls, and bean salads. If you don't like spicy ginger, cut the proportion in half. If you want even more flavor, toss in a garlic clove. A great everyday recipe to make in bulk (this version makes one cup of dressing) and have on hand! It will keep for about two days in the refrigerator.

1 cup water
1 tablespoon chia seeds
1 cup diced carrot (about 1 large carrot)
2 tablespoons grated fresh ginger
1 tablespoon maple syrup
1 tablespoon Dijon mustard
Kosher salt and freshly ground black pepper

▶ In a small bowl, combine the water and chia seeds and let sit for at least 30 minutes, forming a chia gel. When the chia is soft and gelled, in a blender, puree the chia gel, carrot, ginger, syrup, mustard, salt, and pepper until very smooth, about 3 minutes. Store any extra vinaigrette in a covered glass jar in the refrigerator for up to 5 days.

Beet-Tahini Dressing

Beets are deeply colored and add heft to dressings. This is a great dressing for a grain bowl and works well with tough greens like raw cabbage or kale. This recipe makes about a half cup of dressing.

1 medium red beet (about 3 ounces), peeled and diced

¼ cup freshly squeezed lemon juice (from 1 large lemon)

¼ cup extra-virgin olive oil

2 tablespoons tahini

2 teaspoons honey

1 teaspoon lemon zest

⅛ teaspoon kosher salt

1 to 4 tablespoons water (optional)

▶ In a blender, puree the beet, lemon juice, oil, tahini, honey, lemon zest, and salt until well combined and smooth. For a thinner consistency, add the water— start with 1 or 2 tablespoons and add 4 tablespoons at most. Store any extra dressing in a covered glass jar in the refrigerator for up to 5 days.

Strawberry-Caraway Vinaigrette

Fresh fruit is soft, so it breaks down easily, adding vibrant, fruity flavor to vinaigrettes. You can muddle the fruit, leaving chunks of the flesh behind, or puree fruit for a super-smooth dressing. This recipe makes about a half cup of dressing.

1 tablespoon caraway seeds	2 tablespoons apple cider vinegar
½ cup chopped fresh strawberries	¼ cup extra-virgin olive oil

▶ Using a mortar and pestle, crush the caraway seeds until they are broken down into coarse pieces. (If you don't have a mortar and pestle, use a spice grinder or chop them finely with a sharp knife.) In a small bowl, muddle the strawberries until well broken down and juicy. It's okay if fleshy bits remain, but you don't want any large chunks. Add the crushed caraway seeds and the vinegar and stir well to combine.

▶ Pour the mixture into a glass jar, add the oil, and screw on the top. To emulsify, shake the jar vigorously for 1 to 2 minutes. When the vinaigrette is thick and creamy looking, set it aside until ready to use. Store any extra vinaigrette in a covered glass jar in the refrigerator for up to 5 days.

AVOCADO

Avocados are packed with immune-boosting nutrients, offer an excellent source of good fat, and taste great! Making a dressing with ripe avocados ensures consumption of enough fat to keep you satiated. They're a wonderful addition to salads that can otherwise feel light. Make any salad into a meal by tossing it with one of these dressings. A note about avocado—the green avocado flesh oxidizes and turns brown when the air touches it, so we offset this by pairing avocado with citrus. Work quickly and be sure to store any leftovers with a layer of plastic wrap directly against the surface to prevent discoloration. Both of the following avocado dressing recipes make about three-quarters of a cup of dressing—increase or decrease proportions as needed.

Citrus-Avocado Dressing

The fresh flavors from citrus complement the fatty flavor of avocados in this thick dressing. Here, we use both oranges and limes, but you can use any combination of citrus you have on hand. Be sure to taste as you go and add more citrus or salt and pepper as you prefer.

1 large avocado
3 tablespoons freshly squeezed
    orange juice
1 tablespoon freshly squeezed
    lime juice
1 tablespoon lime zest

1 teaspoon orange zest
2 to 4 tablespoons avocado or
    extra-virgin olive oil
Kosher salt and freshly ground
    black pepper

▶ In a blender on low speed, puree the avocado and citrus juices and zest. Increase the blender's speed to high, and with the machine running, drizzle in the oil in small amounts, up to 4 tablespoons, until the dressing is well combined and smooth. Season to taste with salt and pepper and use immediately. The dressing will hold 1 day in the refrigerator.

Spicy Avocado Dressing

Similar to an herb-packed green goddess dressing, this recipe blends herbs, avocado, and spicy jalapeño for a verdant mouthful.

1 large avocado
1 cup roughly chopped fresh cilantro
leaves and stems
½ cup roughly chopped fresh
mint leaves
¼ cup avocado or extra-virgin olive oil
1 medium jalapeño

Zest from 1 medium lime
Freshly squeezed juice from
1 large lime
1 teaspoon maple syrup
¼ cup water, plus more as needed
Kosher salt and freshly ground
black pepper

▶ In a blender, puree the avocado, cilantro, mint, oil, jalapeño, lime zest and juice, and syrup. With the machine running, drizzle in the water in small amounts, up to ¼ cup, until the dressing is well combined. If a thinner dressing is desired, add a few more spoonfuls of water. Season to taste with salt and pepper and use immediately. The dressing will hold 1 day in the refrigerator.

JUICE-BASED

Pressed vegetables and fruit juices can play the role of acids in vinaigrettes. Choose a fruit or vegetable high in acid—berries, tomatoes, and citrus are obvious choices. Combining these with other vegetables adds more complex layers to the vinaigrette. Save a few spoonfuls of your morning green juice and turn it into vinaigrette. All of the following recipes make enough vinaigrette to dress one medium-size salad that will serve four people—increase or decrease proportions as needed.

Green Juice Vinaigrette

For my green juice, I use one whole lemon and anything green—a young apple, broccoli stalks, kale, spinach, and celery work great. If you want some heat, juice a knob of fresh ginger. For something a bit sweet, add a spoonful of maple syrup, which will not overpower the green juice flavor.

3 tablespoons green juice
2 tablespoons oil

Kosher salt and freshly ground
black pepper

▶ In a jar, put the juice and oil and shake vigorously until well combined and emulsified. Season to taste with salt and pepper and adjust. Use immediately. The vinaigrette will keep for 1 day in the refrigerator.

IDEAS FOR THICKENING DRESSINGS

To THICKEN UP A DRESSING AND create a creamy mouthfeel, nut butters can be used. Adding a spoonful of almond butter or peanut butter lends both a fattiness and thickness to dressings. Similar results can be achieved with smashing hempseeds or soaking chia too. Both can be blended into a smooth dressing and contribute healthy fats. You can also thicken a dressing by adding smashed fruit or vegetables. Puree a handful of strawberries into a traditional vinaigrette, and you have a lively, fruity dressing that coats lettuce well. Carrots and other starchy vegetables will also puree into a thick paste, but fat will need to be added. A spoonful of miso lends an earthy flavor that contributes to the umami of a dish.

Rhubarb Juice Vinaigrette

Raw rhubarb is a mouth-puckering vegetable! Acidic like lemon with an astringent quality to it, rhubarb juice is an excellent vinaigrette addition. It's also a wonderful tonic that aids in digestion. If juicing rhubarb, do not include the leaves, which are considered poisonous if ingested.

¼ cup extra-virgin olive oil
2 tablespoons rhubarb juice
1 tablespoon honey

Kosher salt and freshly ground
black pepper

▶ In a jar, put all the ingredients and shake vigorously until well combined and emulsified. Season to taste with salt and pepper. Use immediately. The vinaigrette will keep for about 3 days in the refrigerator.

MISO-BASED

Miso is a thick, salty-sweet paste made from fermented soybeans—an Asian pantry staple. Meant to be a soup base, miso can also be used as a marinade and works beautifully as a thick, flavor-rich dressing ingredient. The following recipes make enough vinaigrette to dress one medium-size salad that will serve four people—increase or decrease proportions as needed.

Simple Miso Vinaigrette

This is a simple miso dressing that can be used to dress greens or noodles—a great basic to keep in your back pocket and then add ingredients to as you experiment more. I like this with a heaping spoonful of smoked paprika. Of course, miso does well with ginger, soy sauce, and sesame as well. Start here and add what you like!

2 tablespoons red miso   2 tablespoons apple cider vinegar
2 tablespoons extra-virgin olive oil   2 tablespoons maple syrup

▶ In a small bowl, whisk all the ingredients until well emulsified. The vinaigrette will keep in the refrigerator for 2 or 3 days.

Nutty Miso Dressing

Combined with nut butter, miso offers a salty-nutty flavor to salads and works particularly well with hearty winter vegetables and grain bowls. This dressing is similar to the peanut sauce for the Root Vegetable Slaw with Salty Peanut Sauce (page 49), and you can use them interchangeably.

Freshly squeezed juice from 1 lime
3 tablespoons water
2 tablespoons white miso
2 tablespoons minced shallot
1 tablespoon almond butter
1 tablespoon minced fresh ginger
1 tablespoon tamari
2 teaspoons maple syrup
1 clove garlic, minced
½ teaspoon sesame oil
Kosher salt and freshly ground
     black pepper

▶ In a blender on medium speed, blend all the ingredients until the dressing is creamy, about 3 minutes. You may have to push the ingredients down if they come up and cling to the sides of the blender. Taste for flavor and consistency. Season to taste with salt and pepper before using. The dressing will keep in the refrigerator for 3 to 5 days.

ACKNOWLEDGMENTS

To ALL OF THE GLORIOUS AND KIND recipe testers who not only spent their own money and took their precious time, but also offered critical notes and feedback that helped inform the entire book—many of whom I know through my fab food community or have been an intimate friend of for gobs of years. I OWE YOU ONE; Jennifer Estes, Jeffrey Correa and Liz Bowerman (shout out to Park Middle School!), Melissa Nyffler, Marta Pasztor, Todd Morris (for the favas!), Marc Schermerhorn, Marianna Stepniewski, Rachel Roland, Euryale Gadin (for telling me my salad was boring), April Smith, Kelly Cline, Chelsea Solomon, Cynthia Nolting Greif, Kira Sorenson, Kate Reingold, Corinna Scott, Hannah Elnan, Scarlett Osier, Mindy Hankins, Erin Wrightsman, Radiance Bellavita, Sonja Groset, Gregory Heller, Anita Vallee, Carilyn Platt (a soul sister), Deenie Esquibel, Emily Naftalin, Gypsy Lovett, Justin Notley, Michelle Ackerman (my nutrition go-to), Tera Beach, Tracy Sarich, and anyone else who helped and I've accidentally left off—BIG LOVE FOR ALL.

I have been in gratitude for many years to Susan Roxborough who encouraged me to write about my passions—gardens and food—and continues to nurture my creative spirit. She is a brilliant, kind soul that I am honored to know and work with. Namaste, Susan. And thank you to the entire Sasquatch Books team, especially Emma Reh for being a stellar editor and Kristin Vorce Duran for her thoughtful and helpful copyediting.

Finally, to my HUSBAND Kenneth Dundas, who in the midst of me writing this book, married me on a sunny day in Glasgow, Scotland, in March of 2016 and then promptly turned to me and said, "Get back to work." Thank you for the gentle pushes that keep me on pace and motivated and for tying yourself to me, and my book projects, forever more.

INDEX

CONVERSIONS

VOLUME

UNITED STATES	METRIC	IMPERIAL
¼ tsp.	1.25 ml	
½ tsp.	2.5 ml	
1 tsp.	5 ml	
½ Tbsp.	7.5 ml	
1 Tbsp.	15 ml	
⅛ c.	30 ml	1 fl. oz.
¼ c.	60 ml	2 fl. oz.
⅓ c.	80 ml	2.5 fl. oz.
½ c.	125 ml	4 fl. oz.
1 c.	250 ml	8 fl. oz.
2 c. (1 pt.)	500 ml	16 fl. oz.
1 qt.	1 l	32 fl. oz.

LENGTH

UNITED STATES	METRIC
⅛ in.	3 mm
¼ in.	6 mm
½ in.	1.25 cm
1 in.	2.5 cm
1 ft.	30 cm

WEIGHT

AVOIRDUPOIS	METRIC
¼ oz.	7 g
½ oz.	15 g
1 oz.	30 g
2 oz.	60 g
3 oz.	90 g
4 oz.	115 g
5 oz.	150 g
6 oz.	175 g
7 oz.	200 g
8 oz. (½ lb.)	225 g
9 oz.	250 g
10 oz.	300 g
11 oz.	325 g
12 oz.	350 g
13 oz.	375 g
14 oz.	400 g
15 oz.	425 g
16 oz. (1 lb.)	450 g
1½ lb.	750 g
2 lb.	900 g
2¼ lb.	1 kg
3 lb.	1.4 kg
4 lb.	1.8 kg

TEMPERATURE

OVEN MARK	FAHRENHEIT	CELSIUS	GAS
Very cool	250–275	130–140	½–1
Cool	300	150	2
Warm	325	165	3
Moderate	350	175	4
Moderately hot	375	190	5
	400	200	6
Hot	425	220	7
	450	230	8
Very Hot	475	245	9

ABOUT THE AUTHOR

Amy Pennington is a cook, author, and urban farmer. She is the author of *Urban Pantry*, *Apartment Gardening*, *Apples: From Harvest to Table*, and *Fresh Pantry*. Pennington has been named one of *Bon Appétit* magazine's Tastemakers and *Seattle* magazine's fifty most powerful players in Seattle's food scene. She has been featured in the *Wall Street Journal*, the *Huffington Post*, *Clean Eating* magazine, GOOP.com, and *Apartment Therapy*. She runs GoGo Green Garden, an urban farming service specializing in organic edible gardens for homes and businesses. Pennington lives in Seattle. Find her at Amy-Pennington.com.